Praise for Clay McLeod C[

Like a demonic angel on a skateboard, like a resurrected Artaud on methedrine, like a tattletale psychiatrist turned rodeo clown, Clay McLeod Chapman races back and forth along the serrated edges of everyday American madness, objectively recording each whimper of anguish, each whisper of skewed desire. This is strong stuff, intense stuff, sometimes disturbing stuff, but I think the many who admire Chuck Palahniuk will admire Chapman as well.

—Tom Robbins, author, *Still Life with Woodpecker*

[Chapman is] a horror-drunk storytelling virtuoso master idiot.

—Helen Shaw, *Time Out New York*

With the trembling voice of Vincent Price and the sinister presence of Boris Karloff, Clay McLeod Chapman . . . uses the macabre to explore the humanity of his characters and reveal an almost spiritual side to the horrific.

—Jason Zinoman, *The New York Times*

Clay McLeod Chapman is like Stephen King transmogrified into a post-punk preacher poet.   —*The Scotsman*

Garrison Keillor on acid.   —*Punchline*

Chapman [is] the literary descendent of Edgar Allen Poe . . .

—*Time Out New York*

If Chapman keeps up with the oddball characters, well-crafted stories, and critical plaudits, that Faulkner guy had better look out.

—*The Village Voice*

Think Edward Gorey. Think Charles Addams. Think Stephen King. But think beyond any of those practitioners of the dark arts. Chapman's pieces go past the macabre, the offbeat, the unexpected, to make strong statements about the human condition.

—*Backstage*

Like a younger, weirder, hornier, and, well, alive Eudora Welty . . .

—*The Village Voice*

A taste of Southern Fried American Gothic that will send shivers down your spine.

—*Time Out New York*

NOTHING UNTOWARD

NOTHING UNTOWARD

TALES FROM
THE PUMPKIN PIE SHOW

CLAY McLEOD CHAPMAN

APPLAUSE
THEATRE & CINEMA BOOKS

An Imprint of Hal Leonard LLC

Published in 2017 by Applause Theatre & Cinema Books
An Imprint of Hal Leonard LLC
7777 West Bluemound Road
Milwaukee, WI 53213

Trade Book Division Editorial Offices
33 Plymouth St., Montclair, NJ 07042

Printed in The United States of America

Book design by Michael Kellner

Names: Chapman, Clay McLeod, author.
Title: Nothing untoward : stories from The Pumpkin Pie Show / Clay McLeod
  Chapman.
Description: Montclair, NJ : Applause, an imprint of Hal Leonard Corporation,
  2017.
Identifiers: LCCN 2016025235 | ISBN 9781495061042 (softcover)
Subjects: | GSAFD: Black humor (Literature) | Horror fiction.
Classification: LCC PS3603.H36 A6 2017 | DDC 813/.6–dc23
LC record available at https://lccn.loc.gov/2016025235

www.applausebooks.com

For Hanna Virginia Cheek

contents

introduction

Celebrating its second decade of performances, The Pumpkin Pie Show *is a literary fist in the face. Part storytelling session, part boxing match, part shamanistic ritual,* The Pumpkin Pie Show *has established itself as an all-points artistic hodgepodge of theater and literature. We pick and choose the essentials of both mediums, channeling their rocking properties in order to create a more intimate relationship between performer and audience. Certain basic rules that we've set up for all our shows are: No sets. No costumes. Nothing beyond the text and the performance itself. Our goal is to strip away those elements that we find extraneous to the tale being told, conjuring up an atmosphere of "creating something out of nothing," as well as focusing on that ethereal connective tissue between the one telling the story and the one listening. Packed with enough emotional intensity to feel like a rock concert rather than just a storyteller spinning a yarn,* The Pumpkin Pie Show *is pure bedtime stories for adults.*

The stories you find here were originally presented in part of the long-running storytelling session *The Pumpkin Pie Show*. The name had popped up in a few zines I'd stapled together in high school, but it wasn't until October 31, 1996, at the North Carolina School of the Arts that I put together an actual show under the *Pumpkin Pie* moniker.

Our first performance in New York City would be a year later for the First Annual New York International Fringe Festival. We were a trio of scrappy Virginia kids who didn't have the forethought to secure a couch to crash on. Our venue owner took pity on us and let us stay in his theater after he closed up shop for the night, as long as we promised not to burn the place down. From there on out, the black boxes of the Big Apple were our home.

Think of *The Pumpkin Pie Show* as bedtime tales for big kids. Think of it as campfire-style yarns with a little punk rock thrown in.

The show's goal has always been to foster an intensely intimate relationship between the performers and audience, which meant doing away with the fourth wall that divided one from the other. To achieve the hyperkinetic level of catharsis these characters demanded, direct address was the only way to go. We want to see the whites of our audience's eyes—while they could stare into the abyss of these characters' murky souls.

Read these stories out loud. Or read them to yourself. They are meant to work both on the page and onstage. Each story is a glass jar containing another rare character, safely sealed inside . . . until you twist off the top and release them. All they want is a captive audience. Someone willing to listen to them tell their side of the story.

CLAY MCLEOD CHAPMAN

NOTHING UNTOWARD

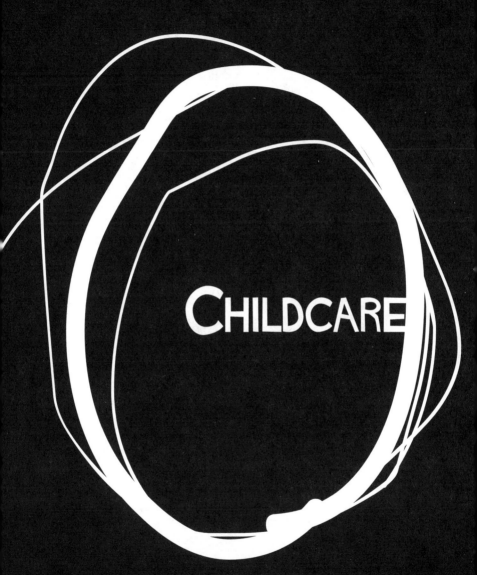

CHILDCARE

mama bird

Shelly's at that age where she'll put just about *anything* into her mouth.

Case in point—just the other day, we were in our backyard. Remember when the temperature finally hit the sixties? Not a cloud in the sky? *That* day. Seemed like a perfect opportunity to let her loose. Explore the great wide open of our own backyard. Lord knows I needed to escape the house, get some fresh air. Shelly's off and crawling across our lawn, tugging up clumps of grass by the fistful, while I just collapsed into one of the deck chairs along our back patio and promptly passed out.

Naptime for Mommy . . .

I couldn't have dozed for more than a minute.

Two minutes, absolute tops.

I open my eyes—and there's Shelly, sweet lil' Shelly, sitting upright all on her own. Her lips peel back to flash me that gummy grin of hers. Total Kodak moment. Her tulip dress scrunches up around her waist just a bit, baring her knees. She's peppered in grass, head to toe, a few stray blades skewering her corn-silk hair.

There's this sliver of pink wriggling against her lips.

At first, I think she's sticking her tongue out at me. But her tongue seems to be struggling. Resisting the rest of her.

Is that a worm . . . ?

No—this is segmented, whatever it is.

Elbowed.

I rush right over—and sure enough, there are shards of eggshell scattered in her lap. All around her feet.

Shelly's gumming a baby robin, freshly hatched.

I see the nest now, perched in the birch just above her head. The infinitesimal peeps of this chick's siblings chirp out for their fallen family member—while the contours of my daughter's cheek keep shifting, ballooning out as that newborn bird butts its head up against the inside of her mouth, struggling blindly to find a way out. One of its featherless wings has wrestled free from her lips, scissoring against her button nose like an undercooked buffalo wing fighting back its attacker.

Shelly Anne Lassiter, I shout. *Get that thing out of your mouth this instant!*

I have to dig my finger in. There's just no other way. Cupping the back of Shelly's head with one hand, I push my pointer through her lips and try to scoop that robin out from her jaws. I can feel the crunch of the hatchling's toothpick skeleton against my skin as Shelly only bites down harder. Biting me now. Her own mother. Felt like a mousetrap made of Bubble Yum and bone snapping against my knuckle.

I yank my hand back—intact, thankfully. Cupped in my palm is whatever's left of that robin, nothing but a knot of pink limbs tangling into one another now. This crumpled mess of wet origami.

Poor thing hadn't even opened its eyes yet, a pummeled sheath of purple skin still sealing them off. One of the eyeballs had popped, dribbling from the lid. I'm getting ophthalmic jelly all over my hands now.

Splendid.

Shelly starts *waaaailing* because I've taken her food away. All the blood in her peanut-shaped body boils up into her head, flushing her cheeks beet red. A slender tendril of drool snakes down her chin as she just keeps howling and howling, a piece of eggshell still clinging to the contorted corner of her lower lip.

Shelly just doesn't understand. Just doesn't get it. One simple rib, one stray splinter of bone could bury itself in the back of her throat and cause her to choke, and that would be that, now, wouldn't it?

That's why mama birds have to chew their babies' food first, I tried to explain before popping the robin into my own mouth, mincing it down into a pretty sufficient pre-masticated pâté for her. *Na wopen wie, hon, wo mwawa can weed oo . . .*

Whenever we do this, I like to pretend I'm a frozen-yogurt machine. Who needs cups when you can lean your head over and pump a dollop of soft-serve straight into your kid's mouth? Just a little game we play. Isn't it more fun that way?

Lunch is served . . .

Shelly's not like other children. She lost twenty percent of her birth weight the week after she was born. *Twenty* percent. All we brought home from the hospital was this shriveled infant. Some freeze-dried baby with all of her body fat wizened away. Skin and bone. I expected some nurse to slip me a set of instructions: *Just add water and—POOF! Your baby's back up to her normal body weight once more!*

She had the thinnest limbs you've ever seen. Her ribs pressed against her chest with every breath. I was afraid I was going to break her if I held her too tight.

Not that I told any of the other mothers that.

I joined the local Stroller Patrol. You know—one of those mommy groups. Just to get out of the house for a while. I needed to see if I was the only one losing sleep. This mafia of mothers from the neighborhood all flock to the local coffee shop, gridlocking the entire café with their SUV baby buggies. Lattes in hand, they all whip out their boobs and breast-feed en masse as if to take part in some massive celestial lactating ceremony. I would simply sit there and listen to the earth goddesses fawn all over their babies—*My little snowflake latches right onto the nipple, my darling angel is already in the seventy-second percentile on the weight index . . .*

Once they realized I hadn't joined in on the ritual, hadn't unholstered my mammary glands for all to see, I'd had to bashfully confess I just wasn't feeling plucky enough to let my kid feed in public quite yet.

I don't think my breasts are ready for their grand unveiling right now . . .

Which was true.

Partially true.

Shelly wouldn't nurse at first. Wouldn't latch on properly. It wasn't for a lack of trying on her part. She tackled mama's ta-tas head-on. I'd find bite marks along my breasts, bruised black and blue. My nipples were gnawed raw until they bled.

Henry, my darling husband—he thought we should bottle-feed her. But, I'm sorry, what baby books had he been reading, exactly? What keyword searches had he done at three in the morning to lead him to this lil' epiphany?

Oh—that's right. *None.* Not a goddamn one.

Don't think I hadn't noticed the stack of parenting guides all piled up on his nightstand table with all the appropriate chapters already marked off with a fine feathering of Post-it notes, all the important paragraphs already highlighted for him in bright, blinding Big Bird yellow—by me—unread, collecting dust, for *months* now.

Maybe we should just bottle-feed her, hon . . .

Formula would be forfeiting. I'm supposed to be Shelly's food source. Not some prepackaged powder. Not some protein shake made by some company.

Me.

I wasn't giving up on my body just yet.

I asked if the Paxil would affect my breast milk. Dirty the dairy, if you will. My doctor promised me nursing mothers only pass on the tiniest trace amounts of their antidepressants to their babies. *So low,* he swore, *it's virtually impossible to detect.*

Good enough for me.

Sign Mommy up, please . . .

I told him I was having difficulty sleeping.

Which was true.

Mostly true.

I had just found a wing that afternoon. A housefly's wing. *Musca domestica*—translucent, webbed in veins. Pasted to Shelly's lower lip.

Now how did that get there?

Shelly had been napping in her crib—still asleep, thank God—so I flexed my pinkie to try and gingerly swipe it away from her mouth, praying she wouldn't wake.

The motion tugged her lip back just a bit.

There. Right there.

Buried below the gumline. A black fragment floating in saliva.

Is that a . . . fly's leg?

So it began with small things. Bugs, mainly. An ant's thorax would dribble out from her mouth. She'd cough up the husk of a grasshopper. One afternoon, a ladybug landed on Shelly's forehead, scuttling down her nose. I was about to flick it away—but instead, I just watched. I was curious to see what might happen. What Shelly might do. I watched that ladybug enter Shelly's open mouth. Watched it descend into the darkness of that three-month old gummy grotto. Watched Shelly's lips slowly seal themselves around the red metallic button of its body and swallow that ladybug whole.

Gulp.

Gone.

Shelly's crib was quickly becoming a burial ground for insect debris she couldn't swallow properly, as she hocked up all the antennas and pincers that got caught in her throat.

But Shelly was gaining weight now! Her ribs sank below a soft padding of buttery baby fat. Her cheeks puffed up, perfectly pink.

My little snowflake.

My baby girl.

Teething had been tough. Her gums grew very tender, very

early on. As early as four months old. Shelly cried herself silly through the night, just wailing away in pain. Henry, *darling* Henry—he could sleep through his own murder without waking up once, so guess who was left to tend to Shelly whenever she got fussy at 3 a.m.?

Bring on the benzocaine!

Our pediatrician suggested I rub a finger slathered up with the stuff along her gums to help massage the soreness away. I'd be lying if I didn't admit I've borrowed a bit of Shelly's prescription for myself now and then, polishing off the tips of my nipples with a little smidge of ointment. Just to take the edge off. A little dab on my temples until my skull was feeling comfortably numb. Then I'd slip my index finger in Shelly's mouth and slide it along that rubbery ridge, just as the good doctor instructed, seeing if I could feel any teeth budding up from below.

All the baby books say the first tooth to usually erupt from the gums is one of the lower central incisors, so I was a bit taken aback by the bony rim along her upper gumline. Hadn't really expected to cut myself on it, either, but—*surprise.*

This didn't look like the kind of incisors I'd seen budding up from the mouths of all the other babies at my mommies' group. The further it emerged from her gums, the more that tooth tapered off to a fine point. Nothing but this slender cone of sharpened bone.

Sure looks like a beak to this mama bird . . .

Prozac is a slower-moving molecule, my doctor explained. *It lingers in the mother's bloodstream for weeks. It'll slip into her milk. There's a risk of developing elevated levels of the antidepressant in her baby's blood, if she's not careful* . . . That's why he preferred Paxil over Prozac. *We don't want to hurt the baby, now—do we?*

I told him the Paxil wasn't working for me anymore. I'd lost my appetite. Lost sleep. Days' worth of sleep. I was afraid of harming the baby. I was beginning to feel a particular resentment toward my husband, who hardly ever lifted a finger to help. All very Googleable symptoms for mothers suffering from postpartum depression.

Which were all true.

Mostly true.

Shelly just wouldn't touch the food I'd make for her. None of the blended vegetables. The mashed bananas. I couldn't get her to eat anything.

So let's say a cricket *just so happened* to hop into the blender while I was about to press *puree*—you couldn't fault me for turning a blind eye now, could you?

The fact of the matter is—bugs weren't enough. Not anymore. Shelly was only growing larger and that meant her diet needed to move up the food chain.

The mice hadn't been all that bad. Much better than grubs. Once you get over the crunch, it's all downhill from there. An amuse-bouche from our own basement. I tried frying them up at first, but *nope-nope*—Shelly prefers her meals *à la tartare.*

The food processor blends them into a pretty pink puree. Nice and warm.

What flavor will it be today, honey? Mouse mousse? Hamster frappé? The choice is all yours . . .

I hadn't realized my prescription had run out until my doctor called. Turns out we even missed Shelly's four-month checkup, which is a big no-no. Now we're behind on our vaccinations and there's a bad flu bug going around—but to be completely honest, I was more worried about our pediatrician poking around Shelly's feathers.

I'd gotten a few e-mails from some of the mothers. *Just checking in, see how you two are doing . . .* Truth is, we don't leave the house that often anymore.

I left Shelly at home with Henry for one last visit to the mommy group. Bid them and their babies adieu. While I was with them, watching them all breast-feed, I wanted to ask:

How far would you go to feed your little snowflakes?

Would you catch their food in a nonlethal mousetrap?

Would you head to the pet store and pick up whatever draws the least amount of attention your way?

If you were really in a pinch and needed to whip something up quick, would you chew their food first and regurgitate it back into their mouth?

What would you do, moms?

I would do anything for my baby girl.

Anything.

I found Henry still in bed. Shelly was squatting just next to his head. From the looks of it, she had pecked out his eyeball. She was tugging on the optic nerve as if to uproot an earthworm, that slender red tendril elongating itself between Shelly's beak and Henry's hollow socket. The nerve snapped—*oopsie daisy!*—the sudden release in tension sending her tumbling onto her back.

We keep Henry in the baby room now.

What's left of him.

Shelly sleeps with me in our bed. I flipped the box spring over. Filled it full of pillows. I padded it out by plucking the stuffing from the couch cushions.

Our own little nest.

Pickings are getting pretty slim in the house now that Henry's starting to spoil. I'll gorge myself on as much as I can stomach before swooping back into bed. Shelly will tilt her head back as soon as I lower mine, my lips hovering just above hers. Nearly kissing each other. She opens her mouth wide as I pump my neck up and down, bringing her meal back up and funneling it into her mouth.

That's it, hon. Be a good girl and swallow it all down . . .

Swallow.

diaper genie

As a father, you think you're prepared for anything. Fevers. Stomach bugs. The worst your baby's body has got to offer.

Then you see it, *actually see* that snail shell caked in crud, and you realize—*No, there are worse things in this world than an upset tummy. Much,* much *worse.*

Poo in the hoo-ha.

Nothing scarier. Taking that moist towelette and wiping away the fecal matter from the folds of my infant daughter's unmentionables is by far, above and beyond, the most horrendous thing I never expected—*never dreamed*—I'd find myself doing.

For those first few months after Tammy was born, I avoided changing her diaper at all costs. You couldn't pay me to do it. That's a real shitty thing to say, I know. I mean, we really could've used the money. But I dodged every dump, I shirked every turd. As soon as that oaky aroma wafted up from her PJs . . . *Oh,* I immediately realized there was an emergency e-mail I needed to reply to, or *Oh,* the kitchen trash needed taking out, *toot suite,* stranding my wife with diaper detail.

Again.

I know, I know. Father of the Year here. But I bet you ten bucks I'm not the first daddy to duck a dirty diaper. And for all you gentlemen out there who've never had to attend to an infant's shit—to you, my good unsullied sirs, I say:

Just you wait . . .

The moment you're faced with your first diaper on your own, *alone*, there's no going back. You don't get to be grossed out anymore. You don't get to be disgusted.

You've got a job to do. So you do it.

And you doo-doo it.

And slowly, *surely*, over time, you're not so grossed out by it anymore. You barely even notice the smell. Because these are *your* daughter's turds we're talking about here. This is *your* kid's shit—and you come to love it, in its own pungent way.

You got to. You just got to.

But yes, Your Honor, full confession—for those first few months, I simply went on autopilot whenever I wiped. Can you blame me? I didn't even look down most times. I couldn't. I'd just lift up Tammy's legs, yank off the old diaper, *wipe, wipe, wipe*, strap on a fresh one—and there you have it. Good to go.

Next.

Sometimes I think Tammy can manipulate her movements. Bend her bowels to blow at her own will, just to mess with me. I showed up to a job interview with a sludgy smudge on my shirt-sleeve, all on account of some spur-of-the-moment diaper change just as I was rushing out the door. I hadn't even noticed until halfway through my interview. This pimple-faced manager started sniffing intermittently, taking a whiff in between questions about my "team-building skills." He picked up on this errant odor my nose just couldn't anymore. My nostrils had burnt out long ago.

Had one of us stepped in dog doo? Did I just cut one in mid-interview and now I'm playing it off like I can't smell it?

. . . Or is that yellow blemish on my cuff a splotch of my daughter's diarrhea?

Ding ding ding.

Didn't get that job.

We're living in a world of shit, my friends. Some of us have just been wading through it for so long, we don't even smell it anymore . . .

My wife blew through her maternity leave. Six weeks. That's it. That meant I was on daddy detail during the day while Mommy went back to work.

Could've sworn Tammy was saving up her dumps until *after* Mom had left for the day, leaving me to clean her up. Sure seemed to me she never pooped *after* business hours. Even her crap got to clock in and clock out.

Was I the only who didn't have a job around here?

I was about to toss out this particular pair of Pampers when I glanced down and noticed something . . . *peculiar.* I'm surprised I even spotted it, it was so slight. A trick of the light. It looked as if there was an indentation running through the poo.

So I leaned over and took a closer look.

Of the three pebbles rolling around the absorbent reservoir of my daughter's diaper, each turd looked like someone had taken a stick and scratched a picture in it.

A symbol or something.

I didn't think much of it, to be honest. Not at the time. I just wrote them off as irregular wrinkles. This was around the time Tammy was turning four months old. She had just barely started eating solid foods. All of the baby books explained that this shift in diet would bring about some funky colors. Perplexing textures. And all kinds of new smells. Her stomach's just got a lot of new nutrients to process. Every poop was a test run, a digestive tryout before she settled on her own signature blend.

Green poops. Yellow poops.

Chunky or runny poops.

It wasn't until the next dump that I started taking Tammy's shit seriously.

This time, there was no mistaking it.

Cave drawings.

Long, curving branches. Some with slash marks. Others with wavy backstrokes. Each turd was embedded with a different primitive inscription.

They kinda looked like letters.

And not English now. No, some *other* alphabet. Much older. Gaelic or Norse or some Indo-European scribblings. This went beyond my bachelor's degree in liberal arts. I was in way over my head here.

But Tammy thought this was all a gas, gurgling on her back as daddy pinched her ankles with one hand and tried his best to duplicate those doody doodlings on a notepad. This was her morning poop, so she'd been working on this BM all night. A real rager. We're talking four sausage links here. One of the turds had been squashed between her butt cheeks, so I couldn't quite replicate the original. I'm not so sure if it was supposed to be an *S* or some squiggly question-marky kinda thing.

Google sent me right to Proto-Germanic languages.

Can you believe this shit? We're talking second century AD here. Elder Futhark Teutonic alphabet systems.

Runes. Fucking *runes.*

In my daughter's stool.

The same angular strokes that were carved into Norse headstones nearly two thousand years ago in the Jutland bogs were scribbled in my kid's shit.

Explain that one to me, Doctor Spock. There's no chapter in our *Baby 411* book that expounds upon medieval litanies written in some four-month-old's excrement.

Felt completely random at first. A scrambled alphabet. So I wrote them down, every last letter, as if they were all part of some secret code I had to crack and my daughter's keister was a fecal Turing machine.

I went ahead and whipped up this little transliterative cheat sheet of Marcomannic runes. I'd found some treatise online—*De Inventione Litterarum*—written by this mad monk Hrabanus Maurus in Bavaria all the way back in the ninth century. For every symbol inscribed in Tammy's turds, I could match it—*nearly* match it—with a correlating letter from our own alphabet. I was off by a couple centuries, so the translations were never exact.

The turds I was translating?

Definitely old-school. We're talking pre-Christianity here. Pre-Latin. Pre–me and my family by centuries.

Depending on what Tammy had eaten the night before, the

pebblier poops would spell out a whole word. Maybe even a phrase. I found myself collecting scraps of sentences. Fragments of something much longer.

Whoever this was, wherever they were, they were trying to speak to me.

Communicate with me.

It took two weeks to decipher the first complete message— *Doomed to an insidious death is he who tampers with this prophecy.*

And there you have it, folks.

First contact.

Tammy's got herself some mystical shit.

As a little experiment, just before putting her to bed, I'd ask her a question—

Any idea when your great-granny's gonna pass away? What's it gonna say in her will?

I'd tuck her in to her crib and peck her on the forehead—*Good night, sweetheart, sleep tight*—and sure enough, the very next morning, the prophecy would be revealed as soon as I peeled back those easy-tape straps around her waist and unraveled her Pampers, as if her diaper were the Dead Sea Scrolls or something.

From there, it was just a matter of transcribing and translating— *Great wealth will be heaped upon those whose kinfolks' flesh now nourishes the worms beneath the earth's own sodden surface.*

I never told my wife any of this.

Um, hon? You can thank Tammy's tuckus for knowing Gram-Gram's only got two weeks before she says bye-bye . . .

Nah, it was just easier to keep volunteering for diaper duty.

Hasn't Mommy done enough already today? Here. Take a load off.
Let Daddy change that diaper.

Things were suddenly looking up for us.

Our time had come.

I had my own oracle. An all-seeing, all-knowing, all-evacuating oracle.

I tried tweaking Tammy's diet just to see if it made any difference in her dispatches. Her main food source was still mama's milk for the most part, which she pumped before bed and left bottled in our fridge for me to feed Tammy the following day—but I'd tinker with the menu just a bit while my wife was at work. Like adjusting the dials on a radio for a clearer signal. Just to see what might happen.

Would any extra veggies affect the memo?

Would fruit further her words?

I learned the hard way to steer clear of too much fruit. Bad call on my part. If Tammy had diarrhea, I was shit out of luck for at least the next two or three cycles.

The consistency had to be solid. *Sturdy.* Moses couldn't use mushy tablets—I knew that now. That meant strengthening her stool. Give her more girth.

That meant a fibrous diet.

I'd crush up an oat bran muffin and pour the reserve of my wife's breast milk in a bowl, mixing them together to make this paste I could spoon-feed Tammy. Maybe lace it with a little Imodium to ensure everything was nice and solid.

A little dessert never hurt—right?

I'd empty a whole bottle of Pepto-Bismol into an ice tray, freezing it. Tammy would suck on those Popsicles until her lips turned this bright neon pink. She *loved* them.

And every night while tucking her in, I'd give her a kiss and whisper into her ear, *What are tomorrow's winning lottery numbers gonna be? Which horse is gonna win tonight's race at Pocono Downs? Any idea which team's gonna win the Super Bowl?*

I bought my wife a Miata.

Surprised her by parking it in the driveway where she always pulls in, blocking her way. Topped it off with a bow on the front hood and everything.

First words out of her mouth?

Where did you get the money?

Like she couldn't believe I'd earned it. Acting like it was dirty. Covered in shit.

Wanna know what the first words out of my mouth were?

Live a little, will you? Don't you think we've earned this? Don't you think I've earned this? Let me be the breadwinner for once.

Tammy's ass had become one of those old-timey ticker-tape machines, unspooling stock info from the future. All I had to do was interpret the data emerging before me. Everything our family had was because of her. Our wealth, our good fortune. *Everything.* I never took advantage of this gift. I loved my baby girl.

My little oracle.

I know how this must've looked to my wife. I can understand how unsettling it would have been to come home after a long day at work and see diapers spread everywhere on the floor. To see me up to my elbows in our daughter's diarrhea.

But what she didn't understand—what you have to understand, what you have to believe—is the messages stopped. Just like that. No explanation. No warning whatsoever. One day, everything's coming in, loud and clear. The next, complete radio silence. Her turds have been as smooth as candy bars for days now.

I wasn't shaking her. This wasn't me doing that. My wife didn't understand—couldn't understand—what she was seeing. I'd never hurt our daughter. *Never.*

All I was doing—all I did—was hold Tammy up with both hands and squeeze.

Just a little pressure on the belly. Nothing too forceful.

Just a squeeze.

That's when the messages decided to come back. Full steam ahead. On my face. All over the floor. Now they wouldn't stop. An endless loop of her poop, saying the same thing, over and over again—

Incessantly plagued by depravity is he who tampers with this prophecy . . .

What it must've looked like to my wife . . . I can't even imagine. Like coming upon a little boy finger-painting with his own poop. The walls all covered in scribblings. The same phrase written over and over and over again—

Incessantly plagued by depravity is he who tampers with this prophecy incessantly plagued by depravity is he who tampers with this prophecy . . .

The smell must've been awful—but by then, hell, I couldn't tell. I'd gotten so used to it, I really didn't even mind it anymore.

Now I miss it.

Would you believe me if I told you I actually miss changing her diapers?

rugrats

You're going to have to forgive me. There's been a bug going around school this week.

I discovered another runny nose in class today. Timothy's upper lip was glistening all through first period. That boy's been sniffling nearly all year. He sweeps his sleeves over his nose whenever there's a fresh dribble. Poor thing's a fountain for snot. His nostrils just won't stop. I can see them trickling from clear across the classroom. The length of his arms will be shining bright under the fluorescent lights by the end of the day, all covered in this petrified mother-of-pearl. Looks like a dozen slugs had a marathon across his shirt.

Use a tissue, Timothy, I say almost every day. *Blow your nose before your clothes are all soaking wet. The box is on my desk, where it's always been . . .*

We were making these handprint turkeys in class this morning, in honor of the upcoming holiday. Placing their palms on a piece of construction paper, the students all draw an outline of their hands, tracing from their wrist on around. I'll pass the safety scissors about, letting the kids cut out their own handcrafted turkeys. Their fingers fan out as feathers now. Add a beak at the thumb and these kids have something to stick on the fridge this Thanksgiving.

For every Thanksgiving for years to come.

That's when I caught Timothy picking his nose. Again. He didn't think anyone was looking, but I saw it all with my very own eyes. And where does his finger go next, but into the industrial tub of Elmer's? Just dips his index finger right on in, wriggling it through the glue. Sally Whitaker was next in line, plunging her pinkie into the paste. Wouldn't be long before she'd want a taste, slipping her finger into her mouth.

And voilà—there you have it. The infection's spread from one student to the next.

Welcome to the petri dish. This classroom is its own hot zone, contaminated with enough kindergarteners to infect the rest of the school. The bell rings and the outbreak begins. I've already been sick five times this school year alone, taking home whatever germs my students bring into class with them. Oh—I have caught their colds. Flew right through their flu. Recycled the same fever I don't know how many times. Just when I think I've gotten rid of it for good, the bug comes back by way of some other student. Same ailment all over again.

Don't worry, the older teachers all say. *Your body will get used to it. Just give your immune system some time to adjust . . .*

Gave some guy pink eye on our first—and only—date, thanks to one of my students. Ended up having to call it a night before we could even order dinner, all because his eyes began to itch. It had been a blind date that only grew more obscure throughout the evening, his eyes suddenly swelling up just after we shook hands. His gorgeous green eyes. Reddened themselves in seconds. His mucous membranes started seeping up some creamy discharge before I could even ask him if he wanted to take a rain check.

We can totally reschedule if you want—

Maybe we should.

Should I . . . call you later on this week?

How about I call you, okay?

Never a second date for me. Not once the school year starts up. Our calendar is divided by illnesses, structured upon the general flow of communicable diseases. Our year begins with that first head cold, moving onto months' worth of fevers. Tummy aches. Head lice. Scabies. Ringworm. Conjunctivitis. Mononucleosis. Influenza.

But we're not here to talk about my love life, now—are we? Of course not.

No, no—we're here talk about Timothy.

Your sweet little son.

These parent-teacher conferences are harmless, I swear. We simply use them to communicate to the parents which areas their children are excelling in. Where there's any room for improvement. Possibly even give some suggestions on how to perfect their performance in school. Now that we're nearly through the first term, we can all talk about Timothy's behavior in class. See how he's been coming along since September.

I'm sure he's told you both how we've been in rehearsals for our annual Thanksgiving pageant. I picked Timothy to play Squanto this year. Talk about an awfully big part. All the kids audition for it.

Not just any student can slip into his moccasins. If it hadn't been for this Native American, the settlers might not've survived that first winter in the New World.

The class has been practicing our songs for the Big Night. Getting their dance moves just right. Half the class dresses up like pilgrims, while the other half get to be Indians, all powwowing around the stage. I always lose sleep the week leading up to the show—sewing together everybody's costumes, making the tinfoil buckles, the cardboard tomahawks. My whole apartment has become some sort of papier-mâché Plymouth Rock, which only weakens my body's natural defenses. I start stockpiling vitamins as early as the first of the month, pumping myself full of echinacea and garlic all day—just to get my immune system up to snuff, come turkey-time. My body's always shot by the time we finally perform, coming down with something or other. Gave my entire family the measles over dinner last Thanksgiving, all on account of Lucy Statler sneezing straight into my face during rehearsals. I had to promise my parents I wouldn't come home with anything infectious this year. My family has officially banned me from the dinner table this Thanksgiving if my temperature is a single degree higher than 98.6. Dad'll have the thermometer ready for me at the front door, just to be sure.

I always tell my kids that Thanksgiving is a time to say thanks for all the good things that have happened to us in the last year of our lives.

Can any of you name some of the things that you're thankful for? I'll ask.

Family, they'll say. *Eating turkey.*

But do you think any of them know that for the very first Thanksgiving a lot of Native Americans didn't have much to be thankful for? Their new neighbors brought along a whole bunch of icky germs that they didn't have any immunity to. Entire tribes were decimated by smallpox.

Can you all say smallpox? I'll ask the class.

Small–pox.

Indians were given infected blankets as gifts from the pilgrims, wrapping themselves up in their own demise. Over ninety-five percent of the Native American population was wiped away by a single disease, never to be heard from again. All gone.

Had a checkup last week.

I've been dealing with this persistent sore throat for a while now. A little bit of a low-grade fever. Nothing too uncommon for this time of year—but for whatever reason, the aches and pains just won't go away. So imagine my surprise when my doctor informed me that apparently I've contracted herpes. Oral herpes. Hence the orofacial infection spread around my lips—see? All the beautiful little blisters blossoming about the vermilion border. The cold sores won't quit cropping up, like a persistent batch of Black Baccara roses budding up from around my mouth. And here I've been thinking all this time that I've just had a couple bad canker sores.

But no, my doctor insists. *That's an inflammation of the mucosa, ma'am. You've gotten yourself a bad case of herpesviral vesicular dermatitis.*

But how? How could I? I haven't kissed anyone in months . . .

Never turn your back on your students. Anything can happen in that emptiness right behind you. Whenever I step up to the blackboard to begin our lesson, I can hear them sniffling. I can sense the snot seeping out from their nostrils. Some kid snorts at the back of the classroom, dragging the mucous back into the chasm of his nasal cavity—but it just dribbles back down. Up and down, like that. All day. These kids are playing tug-of-war with their own sinuses. Yanking on these long ropes of snot. That slender tendril slips down their upper lip and these students just tug it back up into their skulls all over again—and I have to keep on going, *just keep teaching*, pretending that I can't hear a thing. Acting like I can't sense the germs percolating right behind me.

There's no inoculation against these kindergarteners. No vaccination to combat these kids. We teachers are powerless against them. Absolutely powerless.

Say you accidentally leave your purse open on your desk at the back of the classroom one day. Say your ChapStick is just sitting there, exposed to anyone who wanders by. Say one of your own students decides he wants to use that ChapStick, use it without asking. Just reaches his hand right on into your purse and pulls it out, slathering up his lips until they glisten, shining so bright under these fluorescent lights, rubbing it right over that constellation of cold sores wrapping around his lips before snapping the cap back on and placing it into your purse where he found it, before you can even turn around and notice, before the hairs on the back of your neck can stand up, sensing some disturbance in the classroom, never once realizing what's just happened right behind your back—until it's too late. Until there's nothing you can do.

I got herpes from a seven-year-old.

I'll have a friendly reminder of your son on my mouth until the day I die. Timothy's become asymptomatic to me. Just when I'm finally about to forget him, just when his soft face slips into remission within my memory—he'll pop right back up again. He's moved himself into my sensory nerves now, living latently within me for the rest of my life. He'll never go away.

Something red blossomed up on Sally Whitaker's upper lip yesterday. A pinkish lesion just below her left nostril, surrounded by these little flaps of skin. A blister in full bloom. Infected petals flourishing across her face.

I've counted cold sores cropping up on four more of my students just today, all of them within spitting distance of your son. They all sit in a cluster at the back of the class, their desks nestled together. Perfect for sharing chewed-up pencils.

Timothy has turned my classroom into a leper colony.

I keep thinking back to the Black Death. Seventy-five million people drowned in their own pus. Remember how surprised people were when they finally realized that rats had actually been the culprits all along, spreading the bubonic plague throughout Europe?

Now it's children. These rugrats are the carriers. Little snot-nosed savages. Looking at them in their Indian costumes, I can't help but see this tribe of wild children before me, their face paint streaking their cheeks, their bent feathers sticking up from the backs of their headbands, running and screaming throughout the classroom, sticking their fingers in just about anything. And here's your son, head of the tribe, leading them all along. Oh—I've sat him in the corner. I've sent him out in the halls. I have dragged him down to the principal's office and still, *still—he keeps picking his nose.*

I can't even quarantine myself to the teachers' lounge anymore. Miss Henderson, our math teacher—I swear I saw something sprouting up from her lip just this afternoon. A rose petal wrapping around her mouth.

They're everywhere now. I see them everywhere. On everything. There's no escaping them. I tried to tell the other teachers, warning them before it was too late, but none of them would listen. No one will listen to me.

I just want my life back. I just want to be a teacher again.

I want your son to know what he has taken away from me.

I have a new lesson plan this year.

Gather round, kids, I said today, putting on my indoor voice. *Pull out your nap pads.* Nap time always follows right after lunch. I'll turn off the lights and we'll have a good twenty minutes of calm and quiet. The students all huddle together on the floor, slipping off their headdresses, placing their tomahawks down next to them. There's a batch of blankets for the students to use, if any of them want one. Hand-me-downs, mainly. Old things donated from the local hospital.

Still have a scar on my arm to prove that I've been inoculated, over thirty years ago now. I got my smallpox vaccination when I was about your son's age. Hurt like hell. But they say these shots are supposed to last up to fifty years.

On the offhand chance that there's ever an outbreak, I'll be fine.

Ordering the dead pathogen is surprisingly a lot easier than you'd think. All it takes is a fake company name. An e-mail address and a PO box. You don't even need to prove to these gene-synthesis companies that you're a part of some legitimate organization. I can just say I'm a teacher. A science teacher. Working on a class project. All you need to do is order them in portions. They'll send me the custom-made DNA sequences for smallpox right here to this very school—and from there, it's just a matter of me rebuilding the pathogen back together again, from the genomes on up.

You should've seen the kids today. They've never been so still before. So quiet. Rehearsals really must be tuckering them out. The most you could hear was the slight buzzing of blowflies hovering above their bodies, collecting on their heads. They were too tired to even swat them off.

I went over to where Timothy was sleeping, his body balled up under his blanket. His chest slightly rising with every breath— his lungs sounding so shrill, wheezing with every breath. Leaning over, I combed the hair from his face and whispered into his ear, *Happy Thanksgiving, Squanto.*

And then, finally, peace and quiet. Now I could get a little bit of my lesson planning done.

throwing golem

You couldn't have been any older than seven when you first asked me where your name came from.

Remember what I said? *There are only two things in this world that I love more than life itself, you and my pottery—so why not name one after the other?*

The name Clay means "born from the earth."

Which is just what you were. Your porcelain eyes, your sandy silica hair. Even the terra-cotta tint to your skin, all red and slippery.

You were a miracle to me. A gift from God. You needed a name that rooted you to your mother, as if I were the earth itself.

I raised you at this potter's wheel. When you were just a baby, I couldn't afford a sitter, so I had to carry you in a cradleboard along my back, supporting you while I worked. The hum of the wheel's motor lulled you off to sleep just behind my shoulders, letting me keep my hands free to make mugs and bowls. Pots and saucers.

People need to eat off of something. Whatever puts food on the table, I made the plates that held the meal. You always knew which piece was mine from the signature incised along its base. I'd carve my name into the clay with a quill, signed to show that it was an original. Sculpted by these very hands.

The kids at school would tease you over your name every chance they got. Especially after they found out what I did for a living. Calling you everything from *Clay-dough* to *Mud*. Forcing you to eat spoonfuls of soil at recess. You'd come home crying, your lips caked in dirt, wishing you had a simple name, like Jeff or Greg. Something that blended in with everyone else's.

Some names just take time, honey.

You might not've been fond of it in kindergarten, but I knew you'd grow into yours. There's a weight to certain words. Every letter holds its own essence. Mix one letter together with another and their substance combines, adding to the name's strength, until you've harnessed a power that embodies who that person is.

You've created a name that represents their very soul.

And look at yours. Each letter represents a different mineral that man was first formed from. Alumina and feldspar. Kaolin and limestone. The very dust of the ground.

This is what you get for having an artist for a mom, I guess. Always digging for a deeper meaning.

We would have what I liked to call *Clay Days*. We'd set up some card tables in our backyard, inviting all the neighborhood kids over to make their own pinch pots. Just a way to make friends. All the children would gather around me at the wheel, watching me throw. I'd explain the steps along the way. First, I'd take a slab of raw clay and do what's called *wedging*, where you knead out all the air bubbles. If there's a pocket of oxygen trapped inside, there's a risk the clay could explode in the kiln. The heat will turn any excess moisture into steam, bursting right through the walls of your pot. You could lose an entire kiln's worth of work to a single bubble.

A ceramic aneurysm.

I remember you saying you felt dizzy, watching the wheel spin around. When you started to complain about a pain just behind your right eye, I figured it was simply a headache. A couple Tylenol would fix it. But when your vision began to blur, I asked if you wanted to lie down for a while. Take a nap. It wasn't until I saw your eyes for myself, one pupil dilated differently from the other, that I asked all the kids to head back home and rushed you to the hospital. We left in such a hurry, I didn't even think about washing your hands. This crust of clay dust had dried all over them, leaving your fingers looking gray and brittle.

Seven years old and already you had the hands of an elderly man.

The doctor explained that an artery in your brain had begun to balloon out. The built-up pressure was blocking the flow of blood. He tried to describe the procedure to me, what he would have to do before the vein ruptured. He would insert a hollow tube into the dilated artery, snaking it through your brain until it reached the aneurysm—this tiny catheter draining the pressure back down.

He said that there was a chance.

That there were risks involved.

And I remember thinking to myself, *I'm familiar with these risks. Every time I unpack the kiln after firing a load of pottery, I hold my breath, expecting half my ceramics to be shattered.*

As if I wanted him to know that I was prepared.

That I could handle the worst, for some reason.

Four feet, seven inches. You'd never grow another inch taller.

Seven years old. Never a day more.

I made your urn myself.

Looking at the kiln, I couldn't help but think of the oven they cremated you in. Almost expected to find you inside.

The first time I sat back at the wheel after you passed away, I couldn't bring myself to touch the clay. It felt cold to me now. Lifeless. I'd end up just watching it spin around, all lopsided, the clay contorting into different shapes, warping over the wheel the faster I pressed my foot down on the pedal, throwing it off-balance, urging it to move faster, *faster*, until it finally spun off, chunks of clay scattering over the floor.

How could I ever make something as beautiful as you?

What was left in my life to inspire me now?

A potter makes these pieces knowing that they'll hold something for somebody. Food or flowers, we'll never know. But that's what we do. We make containers. Mugs and bowls. Plates and vases. We create the very vessels that hold people's lives together.

A name is a container, too. It holds certain syllables, certain cadences—that, if you say them in a certain order, in a certain rhythm, you are able to invoke the very breath of God.

I wanted to say your name with life again.

I wanted to say your name and have it sound the way I would say it when you were alive, breathing.

I wanted to say your name with all of my heart. To endow every letter with love, everlasting love.

So I decided to make a receptacle for your soul.

I poured a cup of water into your urn, blending your ashes into a thick paste. It became malleable again. It held its form. The marvel of clay is its plasticity, see? Add water and it bends without breaking. It's porous, like skin. Soft and yielding. It has the ability to absorb. To breathe.

I added a slab of terra-cotta and took the wedge to the wheel, getting to work right away. Cupping the clay in my hands, I forced it up into a cone. I pressed my thumb into the center, drilling through the core of the clay, using the palm of my free hand to hold the column in place. I pulled up on the walls by pinching the edges with my fingers, lifting the lip up, using both hands to widen the sides.

Wet clay seeped through my fingers, clumping up at the knuckles. Bits of it flung into the air, the wheel sending sediment everywhere. Dribbles of it spackled the insides of my thighs. It was like giving birth all over again, molding this wedge in between my legs, with my own hands.

I took the time to throw every section separately—hand-building your limbs, rubbing water into your skin until the segments adhered themselves together.

I molded your face from memory. I sculpted your features just the way I pictured them. Carving the dimples in your cheeks. Pecking freckles across the bridge of your nose. I stuck a tiny ball of clay where that mole nestled under your right eyelid. I even carved your scars back into your skin, duplicating every injury you got from riding your bike. Even down to the navel, I added every last detail.

Four feet, seven inches. Never an inch taller.

Seven years old. Now as eternal as the earth itself.

You opened your eyes to me. Your hazel eyes, held up in pools of porcelain.

Your skin was red, as glistening and slippery as the day you were first born. The glaze crackled into a network of veins, running over your body. I wet my hand to fettle away all the blemishes from your skin, smoothing the clay down. I parted your hair with a fork, raking the tines through, leaving behind an even row of grooves across the top of your head. I breast-fed you with plaster of Paris, nursing you to health on slip and gypsum, until you could finally stand on your own again.

When a mother thinks of her only son as her muse, it goes beyond inspiration. He is a revelation to her. He is the one creation that took her entire body to render.

There will never be another. Not like you. So I signed my name along the sole of your foot.

As mother to this masterpiece.

family photos

We're butchered in the first five minutes of the film. The whole family gets their necks slit for exposition's sake, before the opening credits can roll. The kids are fast asleep in their bunk beds, while my husband and I are just down the hall. The television set's still on in our room, casting this blue glow over our bodies. The volume's up just enough that we can't hear the killer coming in through our kitchen window, creeping upstairs. First, he eviscerates the children. Once our daughters are dead, he tiptoes toward our room. He watches us sleep, hovering over our bed for hours, blood dripping off his butcher knife staining our sheets. He disembowels my husband without even waking me up, tuning his entrails like an instrument.

I'd like to think he saves me for last. That I wake up just before the ax swoops down, left alive long enough to gasp, my last breath severed into halves as the blade wedges through my neck.

I suggested it to the director. He seemed to like my idea.

This has been my best role yet.

I've been auditioning for years, scoring bit parts here and there. Nothing really to write home about. I've waitressed my way through this city, serving almost every single casting director I ever auditioned for. They look up from their menus as I'm taking their order, squinting at me for a second before asking—

Do I know you from somewhere?

I used to tell the truth. I had just auditioned for them that afternoon, coming into work thirty minutes late because I had to wait in line with all the other actresses trying out for the part. Most of them just nod their head, smiling patiently as they order.

Something about my face makes everyone think I'm from their hometown. I have "familiar features," I've been told. A modest physiognomy that reminds folks of someone they went to high school with. People pass me on the street and think I'm some girl from their old neighborhood. They look at me as if they should remember who I am, even though we've never met.

Then I got gutted.

The plot's pretty simple. There's a killer on the loose, breaking into people's homes in the middle of the night. A disgruntled gumshoe loses his family to this maniac and swears revenge. Hot on his trail, the detective goes back to the house of the first family and sifts through their pictures, looking for some clue that might tip him off.

Which is where I come in.

I got to play the mother *in* those photos. The director needed to cast a couple actors to portray a family, reenacting these picture-perfect moments.

Birthday parties. Weddings. Christmas dinners.

We wouldn't actually be in the movie—but our snapshots would. We were creating a domestic pretense, a fabricated family life.

No lines, no blocking, no script.

Just smile for the camera.

Just *become* this mother.

My husband had been in a couple car commercials. I remember seeing him on TV before, peddling automotive parts. He had that standard-father face. You'd forget him the second he walked away—but when he was right in front of you, talking about your transmission, you trusted him for some reason.

In the script, we were just listed as "The Lindsays"—so I decided my husband's name had been Jim. While for myself, I'd be Jessica.

Jess for short.

Our girls were just adorable. I learned later that they were actually the daughters of one of the production managers, but for the sake of our family, I considered them to be mine, all mine. Sarah had been born in the backseat of our station wagon en route to the hospital. She was so eager to come out, she couldn't wait to make it to the emergency room. Susan was a little more patient, *thank God*.

We were building a family from the photos on up.

We went through thirty-six rolls of film, condensing ten years' worth of domestic bliss into a couple days' worth of shooting.

Each day, the director would come up with another scenario for us. Sarah's sixth birthday party. Susan's first piano recital. No detail was left unturned. I had to act like a newlywed one day—while in the next set of shots, I had to heft on a decade of dish-washing into my smile, the weight of housewiving welling up into bags under my eyes.

No part is too small, my acting coach once told me. *It is up to the actor to create a history for their character, to develop an entire background that they then bring to the screen. I want to know what they ate for lunch five hours before they're supposed to walk onstage, I want to know when they last talked to their parents before they have their first scene. I want to see this person's life in everything they do!*

To prepare for my role, I'd take Polaroids of myself throughout the day. I was trying to catch myself off guard with whatever I was doing in hopes of capturing the candidness of the moment. Every snapshot had to embody a mom who never saw that psycho coming—which, for an actor, can be difficult. A script is like having a little crystal ball, where the future is only a flip of a page away.

One Thanksgiving dinner, when Jim was cutting the turkey, I caught myself staring at the knife in his hand, watching my reflection pass across the blade. Nobody else seemed to notice. The girls were just darling in their dresses, each of them snitching a sliver of meat off from their father's plate—while I simply sat there, suddenly aware that this would be our final Thanksgiving dinner together.

I called my husband in the middle of the night to discuss some ideas I had for the shoot the next day. Jim listened for a while before saying he needed to go, mumbling to me that we'd talk more about it in the morning. Just as he hung up, I tried asking him about maybe taking us on a vacation somewhere. Just pack up and go away for a week. Just a couple days. One night, even. Anything to get us out of the house for a while.

Susan's ninth birthday was a challenge for me. We'd done birthdays before—but this would be Susan's last. The party took place in our backyard, all of her friends sitting around our picnic table.

Balloons bobbed up from everyone's chair. There was gift wrap billowing in the wind, drifting over the lawn every time a breeze blew through. Sarah got icing all over her nose. There were times when I had to take a moment and focus, trying hard not to project what I knew was supposed to happen a couple months from now. Just as Susan cut the cake, I couldn't help but think about that man crawling in through our window, his knife shining in the moonlight. I'm supposed to be smiling for the camera—when all I can picture are my little girls in their bed, their dreams suddenly severed from their heads. I needed to keep in character, laughing every time Jim made a funny face for the photographer—but all I saw were his lips grimacing, his throat open.

What kind of mother am I for not telling my own children that they'll be dead soon? What kind of wife am I for not trying to save my own husband?

I had to keep this secret inside me. I had to hide it from my own family like a roll of film wound up into a camera. If I were to say anything to them, I'd be exposing the truth too soon—ruining the whole roll with one slip of the tongue, the sunlight eating away at my picture-perfect family.

Once we started shooting our own forensic photos, something had changed in the family. Jim wouldn't talk to me anymore. The girls seemed distant. Instead of resting in the morgue, my daughters were sipping Dixie cups of lemonade in the makeup trailer—their throats painted red, their pajamas soaked in blood.

Some production assistant escorted us into our own home. Into our own rooms. There was red all over the walls now, the sheets drenched in dyed corn syrup. We were told how to lie in bed, the director moving our limbs around with his hands so he could achieve that perfect pose, sculpting that final expression on our faces. As I lay there, the flash of bulbs going off all around me, the director kept calling out for me to *hold, hold, don't blink, hold, that's it, that's it, perfect.*

And for every flash, the only thought that passed through my mind was—*I could've stopped all this. This didn't have to happen.*

For every second, twenty-four frames of film pass through the projector, causing a fluid movement of images. Implying motion. Implying a continuous thread of action. The celluloid slips through the light so fast, the human eye never realizes it's merely looking at a series of snapshots.

I was the photo *within* a bunch of photos. My face was cast across a stream of guncotton and camphor.

My work was done pretty much before the production even started. The cast and crew came into my home, thumbing through my pictures. Looking at my family.

Nobody even knew that I had been there.

I was dead to these people. My life didn't matter to them anymore.

Once the film was finally released, strangers would pass me on the street and suddenly do a double take, stopping me long enough to say I looked familiar. If I actually talked to them, I'd wait patiently for them to realize who I really was, that moment of recognition creeping across their face.

One time, I brought a date back to my place. We were in the kitchen together, fixing drinks, when he noticed the pictures on my fridge.

Who are these people? he asked, pointing to Jim and the kids.

It was a photo from Susan's fifth birthday. Our faces filled up the entire frame, smiling at the camera.

My family, I said.

Family? You didn't tell me you had a family.

They're dead now.

daycare

Edwin pitched himself one heck of a hissy fit this morning. Turned the whole basement into his own lil' racetrack, acting all Nascar on me now. Just ran himself in circles, all on account of snack time beginning at ten thirty-*two* today. Took me nearly ten minutes to catch him. Pull that Down syndrome drag racer right on over.

Isn't that right, Edwin? You made your poor ol' Auntie Paulina huff and puff, chasing after you? Working my rheumatism all up into a tizzy. I'm breaking out the VapoRub in a minute here, you just wait. These gams need a mentholated massage after the workout you put them through.

Susie used to be my masseuse. I swear, there's magic in that girl's hands. But she just can't keep her fingers to herself, now, can she? Always has to dip her pinkie into the Vicks and have herself a lick, making herself sick to her stomach.

You just gotta keep these kids on a routine leash, that's all. Every minute's gotta be accounted for. Otherwise, there's gonna be tantrums. Shit on the walls.

That's why Edwin's in a time-out.

Only as a last resort now. When I've got three other young'uns to look after, sitting him in the corner is just about the only choice Auntie Paulina's got. I pad the pipes with a beach towel just in case the heat kicks on. That way, Edwin won't burn himself too much. Just let him stew there for a while. *Reflect* on what he's done.

Most parents don't discipline their children. Not one lick. Oh, they'll heap a whole lot of "positive reinforcement" on their kids— *You're so good at cleaning your plate, Susie; Look at who tied their shoes all by themselves*—but when it's my turn to look after them, heavens to birdbrained Betsy, lil' Susie here's gotten it in her mentally impaired mind that she's nothing but a princess, wearing a crown of extra chromosomes. And here I am, her handmaiden, waiting at her beck and every call.

I don't know about you, but that's not how I was raised.

I was born into babysitting. Done it my whole life. I was the oldest of eight children. Count 'em: *eight kids*. Just who do you think looked after us while our parents were off at work, trying to put food on our table? If any one of my brothers and sisters ever sassed back to our daddy when he came home, you better believe they were bent over his knee before they could even blink. Then it was my turn, earning myself a raw hide for not teaching my siblings how to *respect* their elders.

Now, I could blow a whole rainbow up your butt about how I treat each and every one of these lil' precious angels with the kind of care the king of Egypt got when he was still shitting in his papyrus Pampers. But this here's an Old Testament daycare: *I have commanded a widow woman there to feed and sustain thee.* Kings 17:9.

After my husband passed away, Auntie Paulina had to go into

business all by herself. Never had any children to call our own. Never needed to. We had so many already. I looked after all the kids in our neighborhood, opening up my doors to everybody on our block, so why not paint a sign over the porch and make it official?

Auntie Paulina's Daycare is open for business.

I had ten kids to call my own. *Ten*. There was Peter. Rochelle. Tommy. Jenny. Julie Ann. Caleb. Christine. Tommy Two. Sally. And . . . ? Almost forgot lil' Wyatt. All of them calling me Auntie. Treating me like family. In a way, I was. Up until Protective Services decided to crack down on unlicensed nursery schools. Apparently, Auntie Paulina needed a *permit* to operate her own daycare. She needed a building *permit* to work out of her own home. Plus a food *permit* to handle snacks. Like some piece of paper is gonna say I'm qualified to serve up Velveeta and Triscuits to my kids.

The state took my family away. Took away my home. Shut me down and threatened to charge me with child endangerment—and for what, exactly? Finding a bathtub full of water? Finding cleaning materials in my kitchen cabinet?

This here was a smear campaign. Just 'cause I hadn't coughed up sixty bucks for some certificate, I couldn't come within spitting distance of these kids anymore.

My kids.

Then I met Edwin.

Everybody's always talking about old souls. *He's an old soul* or *You have such an old soul*. Edwin here's got himself the *youngest soul* I've ever laid eyes on. I'm always saying he's forty-six going on six—don't I, Edwin? Yes, I do. Just look at that baby face, will you? Not a single dark cloud crosses over that concave nose. That broad slope of a forehead. Nothing but blue skies as far as those beady eyes can see.

I first found him wandering along the interstate about five years back. This was when I was still living in Virginia. I asked Edwin here if he was lost and he just pulls out this laminated note card from his pocket. Had the address to one of those group homes for retarded adults printed on it, along with his name: *Edwin P. James.*

Poor Edwin here had gotten himself so turned around, he couldn't find his way back. I asked if he'd like me to take him home. He gave me that grin of his—and I tell you, my heart just about melted. His smile chased all my gray clouds away.

We've been family ever since.

Remember how that saying goes, Edwin? What's it that I'm always saying? *Whither thou goest, I will go; and where thou lodgest, I will lodge.* Ruth 1:16.

A power-of-attorney form is all Auntie Paulina needs to keep this family together. As long as my lil' angels memorize their social security numbers and have a photo ID, those disability checks will magically materialize in the mail every month.

Auntie Paulina's Daycare is back in business!

Basements tend to work best for everybody. They're quieter. Less confusing. In the beginning, when it was just Edwin and myself, there was enough room in my apartment for the both of us. But as soon as Susie came along, I needed to expand.

The cellar was pretty much untouched, save for some soggy cardboard boxes. I taped the windows up with newspaper, for privacy's sake. Found a few abandoned mattresses on the sidewalk, so I dragged them down. I had no idea about the bedbugs until everybody started itching.

I let them decorate the basement however they wanted. Those brick walls were a clean canvas as far as I was concerned. We're talking tinfoil stars. Crepe-paper streamers. And my own personal touch, a posterboard with one of my favorite epigrams: *He who neglects discipline despises himself, but he who listens to reproof acquires understanding.* Proverbs 15:32.

Happy times.

When Susie's federal supplemental security income checks stopped coming in, I had to drag her down to the social service agency and prove she was still living and breathing. Apparently, her parents had put in a stop payment request, thinking she was dead. That was a bit of a red flag waving for this caseworker, no matter how much of a misunderstanding I painted all this as. Took some convincing on my part that this was Susan Russell, the one and only missing Susie Q, alive and well and in my custody—that I was her caregiver and that those social security checks of hers should now be forwarded on up to Philadelphia.

Susie has always been a bit of a handful. She tends to question my every step, so when I told her and Edwin we only had time to pack up our absolute necessities, good Lord, it was as if I had submitted myself to the Spanish Inquisition:

Where are we going?
Why are we leaving?
What time is it?
Why is it so late?

On and on, have mercy. You'd think a family vacation would be fun. *Just a lil' field trip, kids. Now hop in the van and let's get a move on before anyone sees us . . .*

I've made it a rule for myself only to take on new kids when life's at its leanest. But you know how the saying goes: *You can choose your friends, but you can't choose your family.*

Charles joined us just about a year ago, and Stewart came along just a few months after that. All four of them seem to get along just fine. I just have to keep a close eye on them, that's all. They'll wander away if I'm not watching. That's why God created padlocks. Some days, I pray for an extra pair of eyes to pop out from the back of my head, just so I can make sure they don't hurt themselves. Those heating pipes have been hissing and snapping all through the winter, keeping everyone up with their clanging. Poor Stewart here had to learn the hard way not to touch them.

This basement isn't as lavish as the last one, I'll admit. But I never promised the Four Seasons, now, did I? We make do with what we've got. And this is the best we can do right now until things cool down.

The mason jars are just a precaution. Everybody's potty-trained, but Auntie Paulina simply doesn't have the stamina she used to. I can't scale these basement steps every time somebody needs a bathroom break.

I am not the spring chicken I used to be. I've tried to explain that poor ol' Auntie Paulina ain't gonna be around forever. What's gonna happen to them then?

Who'll look after you once I'm gone?

Their families abandoned them. That's the God's honest truth, no matter how bitter a pill it is to swallow. I found each one of them in some god-awful group home, *alone*, with nobody looking after them. Just wilting away.

I saved them from a life without love. I treat them like family. They are my family. So don't you dare try taking my family away from me again.

We're all the family we've got left.

undertow

You got to keep up with me better than this, bartender. With as many sorrows as I've got to drown? I'm gonna be stuck on this stool all night.

Hey. How long's a guy got to wait for a refill around here? I don't want to see the bottom of that glass for the rest of this crisp twenty-dollar bill. We're going to let Mr. Jackson decide when I've had enough to drink. Today was payday, so I'm showing ol' Andrew here a night on the town.

Tell you what. Next round's on me.

How about that, everybody? *Andrew Jackson here is up for reelection and he needs your votes!* He's hired me to personally run his campaign. We're hitting all the bars along the highway, mustering up the drunkards to get behind the wheel.

'Cause on this highway, I'm the worst vulture there is. After the police and paramedics peck through a car wreck, I swoop down for the scraps. This road would be lumping over with rotten automobiles if it weren't for me towing them away—*so don't you tell me I don't know what I'm talking about here.* This highway's *my* office. *You're* the one's walking into *my* work the second you stumble outside the bar.

I've seen what a steering wheel can do to your chest when you hit the brakes at eighty miles an hour. It pushes past your abdomen, your body slams against it so hard. Your ribs grip the wheel, trying to steer. Your heart honks the horn every time it beats—*Honk, honk . . . Honk, honk . . . Honk . . .*

You want to tell me I don't deserve a drink after working around that all day?

I've got two kids at home and I can't even hug them. Feel like my fingers are going to tear right through.

My hands don't deserve to know what that feels like.

I can't trust the touch of things anymore.

None of you know how flimsy your skin really is. *Look at you.* You've all soaked yourselves in enough alcohol, a simple pinch between your seat and the steering wheel could tear right through. But hell. I figure—*I owe you.* All of you here. You boys keep me in business, you know that? Half the calls I get are car wrecks coming from drunk drivers. Makes me wish I was working on commission. I'd stop in here every night, personally buying each and every one of you a drink with the money from my own pocket. I'd earn it all back right after happy hour.

Tonight, I guarantee you, I'll be towing one of your cars out from some ditch.

I just figured I'd come down here first. Pay you a visit before the accident. I wanted to see what you all looked like in one piece.

Bartender . . . Is this a self-service station here or what? *Fill her up, man!* My hands are still shaking. I want to hold my children tonight. Hug them tight. Not think about their seat belts sawing their heads off. Can you do that for me, please?

Can you wash my day away?

I bet you've had to listen through every sad sack's story that's come in here, haven't you? They all line up along the bar and just start sobbing away, don't they?

Bet you think you've heard it all, by now. Am I right?

Well . . . I got one for you.

You fill up that glass and I'll tell you a story you've never heard before . . .

I towed away my wife tonight.

It's true. I'm not lying.

Got the call about three hours ago. The highway patrol radioed in and said they got a wreck down on Route 27, right where the river starts running alongside the road. I was the nearest truck around, so I called the dispatcher and said I'd take it. My shift was winding down, but I was near enough to tow it in no time.

Once I pulled up, I see this winebibber sitting in the road. Man was so drunk, he didn't even realize he'd already been in an accident. He's got this whole entourage of officers surrounding him, asking questions. You could smell the alcohol on his answers—*No, no, officer, I only had a little nip. Nothing to fuss over, I swear . . .*

He'd lost control of the wheel. Skidded over into the oncoming traffic. There was a station wagon heading in the other direction. Both sets of headlights are suddenly staring each other down. To miss kissing fenders, that station wagon had to take a sharp turn, running right off the road and through the guardrail—hitting the river at fifty, maybe sixty miles an hour. You could see how heavy the brakes had been laid on. Half the tires had rubbed off over the asphalt.

I was told to drive toward the water, this officer motioning for me to back the winch up along the shore.

You can't think about the people who'd been behind the wheel when you're on the job. You tow those cars in and you try not to look inside. See what's still caked onto the car. You drop them off at the junkyard and you go home and you kiss your kids good night and you hold onto your wife until you finally fall asleep, *thanking God* you've got a family to come home to night after night. And you hope that you don't have dreams about all the people on the road, imagining what would happen if it'd been someone *you* loved. Someone who mattered to *you*. You pray for a smooth ride through your sleep. No nightmares about finding your family on the highway.

Took me almost two hours to tug that station wagon out from the water. The winch kept winding in, the car getting closer. The numbers on the license plate are starting to look real familiar to me. Like I've seen them before. But I'm not saying anything to anybody. I figure my nerves are just stretched. *I'm seeing things—* that's all. I could go home and find my wife already in bed, curled up underneath the sheets and sleeping. Not right there in front of me. *Whose wife was this?* Not mine. Not with her hands frozen into fists from hammering against the window, trying to punch through the glass as the river swept in. No—*my wife was at home.*

She wasn't out buying ice cream for the family.

It had melted, fogging up the water. It took a police officer to wipe his finger down her arm to realize what she was covered in, the entire inside of the car coated with a gallon's worth of vanilla skin.

Licking his finger, he said, *My favorite flavor.*

Mine, too.

Instead of towing the station wagon down to the pound, I took it home. Parked it right in front of our house. What water was still caught inside was dribbling out onto the road. And I went inside, right up to my children's room. Found them sound asleep.

Let me ask you something. How would you go about telling your kids if something like this happened to you?

Would you wake them up? Sit one on each knee?

Would you wait for the police to ring your doorbell?

Or would you pile what was left of your family into the station wagon and go for a little ride? Maybe head down to your local watering hole. Let the kids sleep in the backseat while you stepped out for a little drink.

I want to know what *you* boys would do.

I want you all to have a drink on me with the money I made towing my own wife—and think about how happy I'm going to be when I pry your car off of some tree, yanking your fender from its trunk.

Me and the kids are going to be in the parking lot here, with the radio on, just waiting for the dispatcher to call in with a car wreck. 'Cause I think it's time they see what their daddy does for a living. See what I've got to deal with almost every night—so that when we hug each other, we'll all know just what it is that we're holding on to. How precious that feeling is.

Tonight, I'm the designated driver. We can all carpool down to the pound together. But first—how about another round? What do you say, everybody?

One for the road?

BIRDS AND
THE BEES

descending the stairway

Sarah Pritchard possessed a particular preadolescent androgyny that left her resembling an eighth-grade Robert Plant.

To the rest of Robious Middle, whispered right behind our backs, Sarah P. had something of an *equestrian* countenance. Imagine a My Little Pony barely at the brink of puberty. But tonight, for the sake of history—for *my* sake—I'd like to look back and think that the ambisexual beanpole that flanked me upon entering the gymnasium of Salisbury Presbyterian had the very same straw-blond locks as Plant. Same horizontal slope of a torso. What prescient twist of fate, what divine rock providence her presence turned out to be on this spring eve of May 13, 1992.

Sarah P., you see, was an "import date"—the daughter of a friend of my aunt's. A middle school ringer brought in from another school two counties over. Because, you see, none of the other girls at Robious Middle had accepted my overzealous invitation to the spring formal—not Shawna Feist, nor Brooke Berryhill, regrettably—leaving me desperate for a dance-floor make-out partner.

Because as every boy in the hormonal throes of middle school knows, these spring formals were merely a pretext for getting straight to first base. No other socially ordained occasion put us in proximity to our female classmates, the distance between our bodies dwindling with each song until that inevitable collision of lips. The jousting of tongues. For the architects of these grade-school soirees had designed a culminating moment of latent make-out provender, that hallowed finale where kissing was practically mandated by the throbbing gods of eighth grade.

This moment is commonly known in most middle school circles as:

The Final Song.

The Final Song was always a slow song, some contemporary radio pop pap. "Giving Him Something He Can Feel" by En Vogue or "Diamonds and Pearls" by Prince and the New Power Generation. But as soon as it seeps out from the speakers, couples instantly congregate within the center circle of the basketball court, ducking under the cover of their dancing classmates in hopes of avoiding the watchful eyes of their faculty chaperones.

Sarah P. and me—we had pogoed our way through a set list that included "Jump Around" by House of Pain. "Humpin' Around" by Bobby Brown. "Jump" by Kris Kross.

Now it was time.

All the boys on the dance floor had loosened their ties, the humidity in the gym thick and buttery with burgeoning adolescence. A certain biological clock was beginning to tick from deep within, its alarm set to ring at the physiologically predetermined deadline of our DJ spinning his last record.

So . . . what would our Final Song be?

Would our brewing libidos be stoked by the immanently makeoutable "Under the Bridge" by the Red Hot Chili Peppers? "End of the Road" by Boyz II Men? Even "Walk on the Ocean" by Toad the Wet Sprocket would've done the job. But no—our disc jockey, sage that he was, having spun his way through countless numbers of spring formals before, chose a selection destined to resonate in our loins longer than any number of these wheezing symphonies from the school year of our Lord 1992 . . .

Seven minutes. Fifty-five seconds.

The Final Song of our eighth-grade spring formal would be none other than Led Zeppelin's "Stairway to Heaven."

Now let's get kissing!

There are three distinct phases one should be aware of when making out to "Stairway to Heaven," illustrated thusly:

Phase One: "The Renaissance Fair"—00:00:01 to 00:04:18

A common miscalculation when kissing to "Stairway" is to simply dive in, tongue-first. This error in judgment will leave you with roughly seven minutes of frantic lashing still on the clock, fatiguing your tongue before you even reach the frenetic stretch of Jimmy Page's guitar solo.

One should not sprint through "Stairway."

Pace yourself.

Think of this kiss as a long-distance cross-country match. Not the hundred-meter dash of track and field.

Page in his infinite wisdom has orchestrated an aural schematic for your mouth to maneuver for maximum make-out effect. From the initial strains of his Sovereign H1260 acoustic guitar, couples are lulled into a succession of gentle pecks with his arpeggiated, fingerpicked chord progression, complete with chromatic descending bass line. When first met with the vespers of John Paul Jones's overdubbed quartet of wooden bass recorders, this tender introduction takes on an antiquated, oddly quasi–renaissance fair aura.

Pecking to this prelude, it was practically impossible not to sense a sudden transformation into something puckish. *Feral.* I felt as if I'd become a Pan on the dance-floor, some middle school satyr in khakis and blue blazer, chasing after the winged fairy of my date across the glen of our adolescence, bestowing her with a blanket of soothing smooches to the accompaniment of lute and fife.

With unicorns.

And dwarves.

Oh—but the tongue doesn't come out until we enter:

Phase Two: "The Quickening"—00:04:19 to 00:05:56

As soon as John Bonham's thunderous drums kick in, innocence is stripped.

Lips part.

A surge of Page's 1959 Fender Telecaster electric guitar sent Sarah's tongue pushing past my teeth—and I answered back with my own. The dam had cracked, releasing a torrent of tongue, flooding into each other's mouths like two pink tidal waves crashing against one another.

But remember: You must—*you must*—rein your adrenaline in. There are three minutes still left on the clock. There are your salivary glands to consider! The need to keep your mouths properly marinated for the duration of the song is essential if you intend on kissing to the very end.

Bonham offers up an olive branch between 05:07 and 05:34. The pulse from his drums provides an appropriate template for your tongue to follow. Mimic the flicker of his cymbals—light, gentle laps to the roof of your partner's mouth. Those thirty seconds of solace from the rhythm section will help sustain your submandibular glands in their production of saliva as you lick your way past the six-minute mark.

Closing my eyes, I left Salisbury Presbyterian behind, transporting myself to Island Records' new Basing Street Studios in London on December 1970.

I'm with the band.

I've become some ghostly roadie, omnisciently witnessing the recording of the track that would forever benchmark Led Zeppelin's untitled fourth studio album, commonly referred to as *Led Zeppelin IV*. Resisting the song was useless now. My head is humming and it won't go, in case you don't know. We were powerless against Plant. The piper was calling us to join him, luring us onto the dance floor, whipping our adolescence into a frenzy with a dizzying multitude of overlaying guitar tracks.

Until, at 05:35, the robust strum of Page's acoustic heralds "Stairway's" final transition:

Phase Three: "Ascending the Stairway"—00:05:57 to 00:07:55

Sarah P. and me—we had gone beyond merely making out. This was no longer *kissing*. We were now playing the guitar with our tongues! They flickered in sync to Page's solo, our fused jaws suddenly becoming the very tablatures of his Heritage Cherry Gibson EDS-1275 double-neck guitar—*as if we were his guitar*! Our bodies fused together at the chest, jaws locked in syncopated yin-yang symbiosis, two contrary forces manifesting a harmonious balance between rhythm section and soloist.

I was John Paul Jones!

I was John Bonham!

Sarah P. manifested both Plant and Page, rock gods made flesh.

Together—our bodies became Led Zeppelin.

But my jaw began to ache with a minute still left on the clock. I could feel my cheeks pulling back to the point of ripping. I was afraid I wasn't going to make it through the guitar solo . . .

But there was no turning back now. The bargain-basement sound system was sputtering bass all around us, reverberating in Sarah P.'s jawbone, as if the song were pouring forth from her mouth. As if she were the one singing to me. And in that moment, in some profound preadolescent way, I knew—*I knew* that I was making out with Robert Plant. *And it felt good . . .* Prompting me to use Bonham's drumbeat to wrestle against the final chord progression.

And then . . . ?

And then . . . Dizziness. A whirligig of diminishing guitar licks slowly winding down. Sarah P. and me pried ourselves apart from one another for the first time since "Stairway" had started. Somehow we had kissed for the entire duration of the song, nearly eight minutes of interlocking lips. Threads of saliva still tethered us together in a web of mingling spit. Breathless. Confused and panting.

What had happened to us . . . ?

What had we become . . . ?

The spell of the song quickly dissipated over Plant's last chant.

And she's buying a . . .

We had stepped onto the dance floor as children, Sarah P. and me—but together, we walked off as man and woman.

Adam and Eve.

Rock and roll.

We exited Salisbury Presbyterian as nothing less than Led Zeppelin itself.

bridesmaid

Excuse me. Can I get everyone's attention, please? I have an announcement I'd like to make . . .

Hey. When I click this spoon against my glass, that means you listen to me, people.

Everybody else got to say something about my little sister. Now it's my turn. I didn't prepare a speech like the best man, here—but that's okay. *I'll just wing it.* If mister waiter brings me another martini, I may even say something profound.

To my baby sister, Sybil . . . May you and your husband have a happy life together.

Mom and Dad always knew you'd make it to the altar before me—but then again, they're not holding their breath over seeing me getting hitched anytime soon.

Tossing the bouquet my way was swift, sis—but save me the favors. Holy matrimony isn't my idea of how I want to spend the rest of my life. Besides, now that you've tied the knot, you're off the hook for good. What do you care about what happens to me? You're the one who's leaving the family.

Say *I do* and *poof.* There goes your maiden name.

My little sister doesn't exist anymore.

She's become some other woman.

But. Before you turn into "Mrs. Peterson," I want to give you a little something. Can I get the band to help me out, here? This is for you, sis.

Try to keep up with me—okay, boys? One and a two and a three and a . . .

"You're so vain . . ."

Come on, everybody. You know the words.

"You probably think this—"

Where'd the music go? I'm not done singing—so why'd you stop playing? I didn't write the song, I'm just singing it. This is just my *interpretation.*

Fine. Forget it. Party poopers. All this white's making me dizzy, anyways. Do you know what a white wedding is supposed to symbolize? It means my little sister's still a virgin. But if she thinks she can get away with wearing that dress, then I must be coming up for sainthood, because I know for a *fact* that that hymen hasn't been intact for *years* now.

A toast to my new brother-in-law!

Welcome to the family, brah. See you at the dinner table this Christmas. If you even last that long. If you ever need somebody to talk to about your wife, then you can always come to me, because nobody knows her better than I do.

And I mean nobody.

Let me tell you a little something about my little sister. She may act all angelic, now—but she wasn't always like that. It's true, I'm not lying. When we were in middle school, we made up this

game together. Just a little something for the boys in our neighborhood. Our parents were away at work all day, which meant
the two of us had the run of the house for hours. Every day after school, we'd pick a new boy off the bus, asking him to come
home with us. Only about a half of the kids we tried to lure into
our house ever came, and only about half of that half made their
way up the stairs—and out of *that* half, only a handful of boys ever
had the balls to set foot into our room. I'd pull the shades down
just before getting undressed, making sure to turn off the lights
before jumping into bed. We'd wait under the covers, me and
Sybil, getting all goosebumply from the excitement. We'd have to
hold our breath to keep ourselves from giggling, trying hard not
to make a sound.

Sybil would put on this really sweet voice, telling him to—*take
off his clothes.*

That was our favorite moment—wasn't it, sis? Remember seeing
them tremble? That slight shiver across the room? Some would
cup their hands over their crotches. Others would just duck their
heads down, burying their chins into their chests. With their
school uniforms on the floor, those boys had nothing to hide behind anymore. Nothing but pimples and ribs, all freckly and trembling.

Sybil'd say, *Now get into bed*—and just like little puppies, they'd
all tiptoe over with their tails tucked between their legs. We'd
make them lie down in between us. Pulling the covers over ourselves, we'd keep on our backs, shoulder to shoulder to shoulder,
our arms the only parts of our bodies touching one another.

But that was enough. There was enough friction within our skin to make my breathing deepen. I could always get a sense of Sybil on the other end of this boy, whoever he was, the current of her person passing through his body, making its way into me . . .

Hey, mister waiter—aren't my parents paying you to cater this party? I need another refill. I can feel my lips again, which means I need another martini—*now.*

Because I want to talk about . . .

Billy.

Everybody remember little Billy Pendleton? You should. It's not as if he lived down the street from us for thirteen years or anything. It's not as if he was our *neighbor* for half of our lives. Little Billy Pendleton had a crush on Sybil here, but she treated him like shit all through middle school. *He's too easy,* she'd say. *Where's the fun in bringing him home?* But then, one day, I had to stay after school for detention, only to come back to the house and find *him* under the covers. Little Billy Pendleton's wrists are tied to my bedposts! He's pleading with me, begging me to let him loose. Just when I start to untie the knot around his left hand, Sybil comes walking back into the room, hefting our father's toolbox. She drops it on the floor, screwdrivers and nails rattling inside. Jumping onto the bed, she pushes me away.

Don't let him go, she says. *We've haven't even started yet.*

Pulling the covers away, I see that he's naked. The stretch of his chest is covered in bruises. *Hickeys.* He's got a trail of *hickeys* sprinkled all over him! The blood vessels burst just beneath the sheath of Billy's skin. The negative space between my sister's lips were imprinted all across his body.

Still had his tighty-whities on. There was just barely a bulge.

Less than a lump, really. More like a pimple? The merest hint of cotton stretching beyond its normal proportions.

Pull his undies off, Sybil said.

Why? I asked.

Because I want to try something new, she said, pulling out a pair of pliers from dad's toolbox.

We kept all of Billy's pubic hair in an empty mayonnaise jar, collecting the remnants of his prepubescence. In the name of grade school science, Sybil was determined to learn what made little boys like little Billy Pendleton tick. She wanted to cut him open just see the snakes and snails and puppy dog tails come spilling out, squirming across our bedspread—while I just stood by her side, *her own little Igor,* devoted to the very end.

Billy's face started popping up on telephone poles. I'd see his yearbook picture flickering by on the bus ride to school. I'd look out the window and there he'd be, zipping past. One morning, I nearly choked on my cereal, finding him staring right at me from the back of our milk carton. *Little Billy Pendleton.* All scrawny and meek. The additional bits of his body beginning to stack up inside our closet. Jars full of hair, teeth. Whatever Sybil could pull. And when he stopped responding to her experiments, she got bored with him quick. His refusal to flinch at her pinches was beginning to piss her off—'cause she wanted to keep playing.

That's the problem with these boys, sis. They give up before us girls are finished, leaving us with a need they can't fulfill. Am I right? I thought you would've figured that out with your little after-school laboratory. They quit too quickly. They'll abandon you before you're through.

Marrying them won't make much of a difference, I promise. This guy's not going to be any different from the rest. And I'll tell you this, sis—I don't think I'm going to be there to help you out with this one. I'm tired of coming to your rescue every time you're through. When we were younger, I would've done anything for you. I was the one who dug the hole in our backyard, I was the one who buried Billy beneath our swing set. I never said anything to anybody about him.

Every secret you ever shared with me, I kept them close, making them sacred, believing it meant as much to you as it did to me.

It always boiled back down to you and me, sis.

Until now.

Until you said *I do* to this lab rat. What makes him different from the rest?

What can he teach you that the others didn't?

What can *you* learn from *him* that's making you leave *me*?

I caught the bouquet today, which means I'm supposed to get married next. But I'd never let my work get the best of me, sis. Fucking with the test subjects has always been your department. Me—I just clean up your mess once you're done.

And fuck it if you think I'm following you on your honeymoon.

late bloomer

We all saw it sprawled across the blackboard the second we stepped into Miss Lovecraft's class. Its wingspan reached from one end of the room to the other, hovering above our heads as if it were about to pounce—its chalk-scrawled claws looking ready to grab up an unsuspecting student and fly away.

Its mouth hung low to the ground, donning an outward set of lips that hid a much smaller pair—both of which were peeled freely back in order for the class to stare down the diagram of its cavernous throat.

It must suck its prey up from below, I thought, *like a bottom-feeder feasting off the murky ocean floor . . .*

Its sole sense of perception stemmed from an antenna protruding out from the top rim of its inner lips. That slimy appendage would slither out from its mouth, like a snail easing up from its shell, searching blindly for its next victim.

What is that ungodly thing? my best friend, Jimmy Pickman, asked.

It looks like an octopus, I replied.

Miss Lovecraft had scribbled its name over its dome-shaped

head, beckoning the class to chant out this creature's nauseating nomenclature.

Now, class—repeat after me. This is . . . the vagina.

I shuddered at the sound its name made within my mouth, whispering it with the rest of the students! It seemed to seep out from over my tongue, the syllables all soft and moist, as if it had just dredged itself up from some sordid portion of my stomach, buried for centuries under the muck of my meals, rising up toward my teeth on a tide of bile.

Now, class—all girls are born with a vagina. *The* vagina *is home for the* uterus—*shown here—where the fertilized* ovum *develops into a* fetus.

And suddenly it struck me.

The more we all called out its name, repeating our gym teacher's incantation for this feminine effigy, the more I realized how all the girls in class had begun to shift within their seats. Noreen Dunwich popped her Hubba Bubba right into my ear, the air hissing out from that gummy bubble like a dying man's final exhale. She had been voraciously taking notes, recording every pagan name her high priestess called out! I peered underneath her desk—only to find her legs spread wide open, her knees fanning back and forth . . . Something had awoken within her! Something was lurking under the murk of her skirt, veiled behind the pleats of her school uniform!

This wasn't sex ed. No—we were taking part in something much darker than our normal curriculum.

This—this was a ritual!

An invocation of evil!

As I looked back at the blackboard, that powdery rendition seemed to come alive. Its fallopian tubes undulated across the wall, like tentacles reaching out for me! There was something so hypnotic about its flickering, those ovaries pulsing in a brilliant pink and green. My eyes raced around the room, the sudden shock of realization dawning on me . . . This quivering deity that Miss Lovecraft had mapped out on the chalkboard *was within women*! *Women, everywhere!* These ancient beings had been amongst us boys all along, hidden within the depths of our female classmates!

Now, class—let's move onto the male sexual organs . . .

Bear in mind, I had not known such a thing existed within me. To say that a mental shock was the cause of what I inferred—that last straw of sanity snapping as Miss Lovecraft took her chalk and etched a most heinous hieroglyphic across the blackboard—is to ignore the simplest bit of my experience. Maybe a madhouse would be as good a place as any to save me now. A doctor could erase this profane image from my brain forever . . . For I found myself staring at none other than Him Who Is Not to Be Named, The Mighty One-Eyed Messenger, The Goat with a Thousand Young!

Stop snickering, children . . . I'll report you all to the principal if you can't act like mature adults. Now repeat after me. This is . . . the penis.

You must believe me, Principal Peters . . . I have certain evidence that monstrous things do indeed live within the dark corners of man (that have yet to be explored with my hands). Throbbing, *pulsating* creatures that inhabit a space unfamiliar to this particular seventh grader . . . And as God is my witness, how I wished to resist this transformation! I was the caterpillar combating its own cocoon!

Looking around the room, I realized I was not alone in this chrysalis state. The rest of the class was undergoing the same change, a look of utter horror frozen on everyone's face.

Locking onto the eyes of Larissa Innsmouth, I was suddenly aware of the disconnected sounds inside my mind. The creature hidden within her was attempting to communicate with me! Its sole mode of speech were a series of thought waves, transmitted through its clitoral antenna. Even now these beasts talked in their tombs, sending their telepathy out from beyond the cotton lining of all the girls' underwear . . .

The panic was lessening within me. I was beginning to feel *queerly drawn* toward the unknown sea-depths of my female class-mates. I suddenly felt the compulsion to swim toward that brood-ing reef of newly grown pubic hair, diving into that black abyss *foreeeeeeever*!

Miss Lovecraft was responsible for introducing us boys to the female reproductive system! Her incantation had unlocked our li-bidos. Pushing our desks together, we created an altar in which to enact our rites of passage. The class made sacrifices out of our-selves, offering our bodies up to our idols. Miss Lovecraft con-tinued to point toward the orifices of our gods, while the student body had an orgy of ungodly proportions!

Hail, Yog-Sothoth, the Mighty Vagina!
Praise the pit of shoggoths!
Glory to the Great Messenger, Cthulhu!
Yuggoth, the cyclopic worm!

You mustn't think I'm mad, Principal Peters . . . There's good reason, God knows. I'm lucky enough to still have a scrap of sanity left within me. I have borne witness to terrors that come from beyond the body. Monstrous things that dwell inside the shells of men—like you. And I.

The rest of the seventh grade may not believe me—but later, my peers will weigh each statement I made as I was dragged down the hall, correlating my words with the known facts, no matter how raving, until the entire class asks themselves *how* they could have believed otherwise.

Until then—I myself saw nothing but *madness* in these wild tales I have acted on. Even now I ask myself whether I was misled—or whether I am not mad at all . . .

But.

The second my knees buckled upward, hitting the underbelly of my desk, the rest of the class all turned around to face me. Even Miss Lovecraft was staring at me, her mouth hanging wide open, the look on her face thickening into utter horror as soon as she realized my pants were now crumpled up at my ankles. My hands hidden below the desktop. Strips of mother-of-pearl stretched along the floor, as if some slimy beast had been released from within me, the residue of its escape shining over the linoleum!

gladiatorum

A wrestler has been identified as the possible source of a skin herpes outbreak that prompted Minnesota high school officials to impose an eight-day suspension of wrestling competitions and contact practices.

—ASSOCIATED PRESS, 2007

No jerking it before a tournament. Coach says a champion only chokes his chicken when he's got something to celebrate, popping his top *after* he comes home with the trophy. Never the night before. You want to build up that tension in your body. Harness every fluid ounce of testosterone your testicles can brew, until you feel like you're going to explode all over the mat—just like shaking a can of Coors before shotgunning it, your balls nearly about to burst with all that pent-up aggression.

Keeps you sharp. Keeps you *mean.*

None of us are touching ourselves the week leading up to regionals. Hands off for the whole team. And if you've got yourself a girlfriend, well, you better just let her know loud and clear that there's a moratorium on heavy petting until we come home with the state title.

Just because there's a standstill on hand jobs doesn't mean you're not allowed to provide me with a little pleasure now and then, my girlfriend huffed.

Coach says it's bad luck to munch carpet before a tournament.

Maybe for you—but I'm not on the wrestling team.

Sweat was pebbling my forehead before the ref even blew his whistle. Headed down my brow, right into my eyes. The salt instantly started to sting. Burned the sight right out of me, blurring everything. I couldn't focus on my opponent for more than a few seconds before my retinas began to bite. All I could see in front of me is this spandexed silhouette, this flash of blue Lycra circling around me the instant the whistle spits into my ear. This featherweight motherfucker from Flathead, Montana, was suddenly grabbing at my ankles. He gripped onto my left foot and lifted it up to his waist, trying to take me down—so I just went ahead and threw my whole body backward, hefting the rest of my weight upon him. Let gravity take it from there. We both go down, him leading the way. All 152 pounds of myself pancaked my opponent flat against the mat like a stack of flapjacks, the syrup of our sweat shattering off our skin the second we make impact.

I am the Singlet of Red-Spandexed Death!

I am the avenging hand of God!

The crowd leapt to their feet as soon as the ref raised my hand over my head, christening me the winner. There's my girlfriend, yelling her head off at the back of the bleachers. She's brandishing this banner she'd made out of posterboard—

Revelations 6:17. The great day of His wrath has come.

Every *o* looked more like a Magic Markered heart from where

I was standing. I just spat out my mouth guard and smiled, watching the plastic bit spiral through the air like it was the translucent horseshoe of Pestilence himself.

Damn well better believe the day of reckoning was upon us right here in my hometown of Rochester, Minnesota.

Clash Duals. One of the top tournaments in the whole country. Thirty-two teams from thirteen states. Hastings High. Skutt Catholic. Iowa City West. Nothing but the best. All state qualifiers as far as the eye could see, filling up every inch of mat space inside the Rochester Sports Center.

Friday kicked off with a qualification tournament, round-robining through the pool of schools until the winners moved on into the championship bracket.

Division One, baby! We're talking gladiators here. *Fuck* the runner-ups. They were as good as going home empty-handed before the first day was even over.

Oh, I'm sorry, Coach had barked at us back in the locker room. *Did you come all this way for some fifty-cent piece-of-shit plastic trophy?*

No!

Is this all about getting your name in the school newspaper?
No!

No—you want to own your opponent! You want to get biblical on this son of a bitch! Relent the wrath of God upon him! You want him to crawl off that mat with a little reminder of just who it was that took him down! A memento that he's gonna carry around for the rest of his life! So? What the hell are you waiting for?! Get out there and give him something to remember you by!

The first cold sore cropped up on Danny Patton's lower lip in Birmingham, Alabama, about a week after the Clash. Nothing more than a pinkish lesion orbiting the vermilion border of his mouth, as innocuous as any pimple that had ever sprouted there before. But by the time the morning bell rang, another fever blister had already risen right up from where his upper and lower lips met—a creamy mushroom cap nestling itself directly inside the bow of his mouth. By lunch, Patton practically had a whole crop of cold sores breaking through the surface of his skin. His wrestling coach took one look at his face and refused to even let him practice, quarantining him to the clinic instead. Let the school nurse figure out just what the hell it was that was happening to this kid's skin.

Danny Patton had lost the coin toss to me.

I'd opted for the bottom position, opening our second-period match at the Clash on my hands and knees. The scent of collective sweat had thickened itself into the afternoon, the humidity of the auditorium increasing with each match. Over a hundred struggling bodies were all slathering themselves up in each other's sweat.

Got to be quick off the whistle.

React faster.

Got to pop off the mat, leap to my feet.

Got to explode before my opponent's first movement, wrap my arm around his leg. Take him down before he can force me to the floor.

If you want to wrestle at a competitive level by the time you're a freshman, you better hit that mat as early as junior high. I can remember Coach marching into my middle school, looking to recruit students for his summer wrestling camp. Get us while we're young. Fresh meat for the mat. He stood before my entire gym class and told us point-blank: *Football's for pussies. Basketball's for faggots. You want to be the most physically fit athlete in school? Want to become tougher? Earn respect? Try wrestling.*

I had never sweat before. Never perspired to the point of smelling myself. But listening to Coach Haversand, all twelve years of myself—it was like the BO just broke right on out of me. Puberty was upon us all, as if the coach was Moses or something, summoning up the sweat from our bodies with nothing but his voice.

The hell do you want, kid?

To wrestle.

Not for the next four years, you're not . . .

Standing defensive position. That's how I spent my summer. Legs outspread. Hands out front. Coach would take five steps back from me, bouncing this worn-down tennis ball in his hand. The second he'd pivot, he would lob that ball directly at my legs. Struck me square in the lats all summer long.

React to the ball, goddamn it! he'd yell. *Block it before you're hit!*

Practice wasn't over until I had crumpled onto the mat. A couple other kids from camp would have to come pick me up, slinging my arms over their shoulders and dragging me back to our cabin.

Always heard that hollow *thwonk* reverberating through my ears well past practice, no matter where I was. In the cafeteria. In the showers. Just behind my back. I'd wake up in the middle of the night in a cold sweat, swearing to myself that I just heard a tennis ball bouncing next to my bunk.

But you better believe my lats were conditioned to wrestling perfection by the end of the summer.

Only six hundred and thirty-eight more muscle groups to go.

I'm going 41 to 0 my senior year. Eight straight wins last month alone. Already set the record for the state before I even graduate. I've won for my weight class two years running now. I'm finishing my high school career with eighty-seven pins, a hundred and one wins.

Fucking rabid for the mat is what I am.

Nobody can take me down.

We need to talk, my girlfriend said. *Is there something you want to tell me?*

Not really.

I found something this morning.

Found what?

. . . On my lip.

I spotted my first cold sore starting up my car last week, just before heading off to the Rochester Sports Center. I'd flipped on the radio when something red caught my eye in the rearview mirror. I just sat there with the engine idling in my driveway for Lord knows how long, staring at my reflection. Counting and re-counting the cold sores clustering around the right side of my face.

Coach makes us memorize the medical guidelines for statewide wrestling when we're freshmen. I knew the rules: *No oozing.* If you catch some kinda skin rash, you need to be symptom-free for at least ten days before you can compete again.

I had three hours.

Foghat's "Slow Ride" started seeping out from the speakers. I looked over to my gym bag, resting next to me on the passenger-side seat. I pulled out my jockstrap and began flagellating myself with it, whipping in time to the guitar riff, lashing at my back with the elastic right there in the car.

I prayed. I prayed, beseeching Jesus in my Chevy.

Please. Scourge my skin of this sickness. Please take these lesions away. Just let me wrestle. Just let me wrestle one last time . . .

Slow ride, the radio sang.

Take it easy, I prayed.

Word just got back that Saint Lazarus Academy, only two counties over, closed its doors today after three of its students came to school this morning with several red vesicles enveloping their extremities. Panicking parents have been pulling their kids out from class before they catch it, whatever this was.

Wasn't just Minnesota. This was crossing state lines. Alabama. Nevada. Montana. The symptoms are the same, no matter where they pop up. Sore throats. Swollen lymph nodes. A slight tingle in the skin before the lesions start to rise.

Herpes gladiatorum. Same strain as the herpes simplex type 1 virus.

One touch is all it takes. A little skin-to-skin contact between wrestlers and the damage is done.

Twenty-seven athletes so far. Eleven different wrestling teams from eleven different schools. Seven separate states and counting, all diagnosed with the exact same skin rash.

Our classrooms have become leper colonies now.

All because of me.

I am Wrestler X. My mouth is ground zero.

I am the pestilence sent as retribution for our athletic iniquities! I will hold illimitable dominion over every match from here to the Final Four Championships!

Principals all over this country will have to explain to parents just why it is their sons will never wrestle again once I'm through with them. Because if you want to hit your opponent where it counts, where it really hurts—you got to take it all away. Strip them of their hope. Their college scholarships. Their goals of ever going into the NCAA. Down to the very nerve endings. *Everything.*

Until there's nothing left.

Nothing at all.

Nobody beats an outbreak. Until there's no one left to infect, there's no stopping it. It's just a matter of how many wrestlers the virus takes down with it before burning itself out.

condo lothario

Doctors said sexually transmitted diseases among senior citizens are running rampant at a popular Central Florida retirement community.

—LOCAL 6 NEWS, ORLANDO, 2006

Betty Reynolds simply cannot cover up her chancres with liquid concealer and pray those pustules just *go away*.

None of the nurses here seem to've noticed, or dare I say *care to*—but when Betty made her way into the cafeteria this morning, sitting herself amongst the rest of us ladies, it was practically impossible not to spot the ruddy lumped lesions lining her nostrils. Herpes at seventy-six is most certainly inconceivable—*but there it is, people*, staring right back at us. Even underneath all that foundation of medium beige pancaked across her face, there's no denying the disease now.

Now—we can all add Betty to his list of conquests.

Another mark carved into the bedpost of our own residential lothario . . .

Mr. Talbot.

Toss Laurel Pritchard's chlamydia into the mix and it would appear that we're in the midst of an outbreak here. Our own sunny little retirement community has suddenly turned itself into a senior-citizen Sodom and Gomorrah. Each interlocking condo is host to its own depraved bacchanalia.

I blame the blue pill.

(*Viagra.*)

Before our pharmacist started doling out prescriptions of sildenafil to the gentlemen here, a lady never had to worry over catching the clap. Now you can always hear those tinfoil packets rattling about in their pockets. *Never leave your rooms without it*—do you? Watch you all pop a pill before Game Night begins and you boys bring back the blood flow in your britches quicker than you can call—

Bingo!

But we are not your concubines, *thank you very much.*

Just because there are far fewer men here doesn't turn this nursing home into your harem. Us ladies have lived long enough, lived *through* enough, to earn a little more respect than to be treated like *pieces of meat* past their prime.

As if being abandoned by our families wasn't bad enough. Luring us all into this place with promises of *simply picking up a pamphlet.* Completely harmless. But it's a trap! One moment, you're only getting the grand tour. But as soon as your back's turned—*poof*—your daughter's gone. Your own home's been sold right out from underneath you, *right behind your back*, swapped for some nondescript condo.

Suddenly you're signed up for line dancing in the cafeteria.

Aerobics every Wednesday.

Macramé.

Pokeno.

Bingo.

Dominoes.

You're stranded here, put out to pasture with all the other parents nobody wanted anymore.

And then, right out of the blue—your urine begins to burn.

Feels like a brushfire in my britches every time I sit on the toilet seat. These pains have been pummeling my pelvis for months now.

But no doctors. Certainly not the ones on staff here. These walls are far too thin. The last thing I've wanted was the women here whispering about matters that are of *no concern* of theirs to begin with. If you don't mind: *Mind your own business, thank you very much.*

I was sixty-five when my husband had his heart attack. *Sixty-five.* See the photograph of that much younger woman there? Beaming in her bridal gown? Nothing but a butterfly pinned beneath its glass case, framed and dried.

Bachelors are such an endangered species in these retirement communities, outnumbered by us women four to one. The demand for an unmarried man is so steep, we tend to compete for these gentlemen's affection. These Thursday night social mixers are nothing more than a tug-of-war amongst us widows. Watch us all scramble over the scraps on the dance floor like a rabid pack of hyenas bickering over eighty-year-old carrion—*He's mine! No, let him go! I was here first!*

How utterly unbecoming. You wouldn't catch me participating

in these feeding frenzies. The thought of meeting someone new at my age was just absurd.

Is this seat taken?

Do I have much choice in the matter? I asked back.

Mind if I join you, then?

It's a free cafeteria the last time I checked.

The devil was never this debonair. Always with the pin-striped suit. The fresh flower pinned to his lapel, snipped from our very own garden. And the look he'd give you? Good heavens. *Watch out, ladies* . . . The rest of the cafeteria may as well have melted away once he set those baby blues on you, believe you me.

My name is Nathaniel, he said, extending his hand. *Nathaniel Talbot.*

Mr. Talbot lost his wife to cervical cancer nearly thirteen years ago now. Hearing him talk about their forty-one years together, it was impossible not to think of Walter. Would you believe me if I told you I was worried half to death that my husband was watching this all unfold, somehow? Looking down at me from heaven above as I made an absolute fool out of myself? Poor Walter had to witness his wife stumble through this clumsy courtship with some other gentleman, blushing like a little schoolgirl on the playground after all these years . . .

What he must've thought of me—I don't even want to imagine.

Forgive me, Walter . . .

But an idea had blossomed in my mind. The *what-if* of it all. *What if* I actually relented? *What if* I accepted Mr. Talbot's advances? *What if* I started a second life for myself here, with what little life I had left to offer someone else? Someone new?

I fear we're being watched, Mr. Talbot whispered.

Sure enough, Wendy Pendleton and Laurel Pritchard were eavesdropping on us from the neighboring table.

They're just jealous, I said. *Back off, ladies! Sink your claws into someone else!*

Care to go somewhere more . . . private?

Forward now, aren't we?

Why put off till tomorrow what we can do tonight?

With an attitude like that, I huffed, *you could kick the bucket before tomorrow even comes.*

Your condo . . . or mine?

Mr. Talbot's penis was appalling. I'm being frank here, forgive me, but I believe I've earned the right to be as candid as I can be. I hadn't seen a gentleman's genitalia for years. *Years.* I daresay I'd almost forgotten what they looked like. Definitely never remembered them looking as withered as this—but there it was, flopping before me like some shriveled chicken neck partially plucked of its salt-and-pepper feathers. How it would ever rise to the occasion was most certainly beyond me.

Have no fear, Mr. Talbot said, popping a cobalt diamond directly into his mouth. *Nothing a little pharmaceuticals can't cure . . .*

Care to guess how many sexual partners I had before our venerable Mr. Talbot?

One. God rest his soul.

Why on earth would I ever worry over protection when pregnancy was most certainly no longer a concern? No need for condoms after menopause, now—is there? I couldn't have found a prophylactic in here anyhow, had I torn this place apart, top to bottom—let alone even know how to slip one on somebody's willy.

I'm a little rusty at all this, I said. *Forgive me. It's been a while.*

Don't worry. We can take this as slow as we want.

Not too slow now. Don't want you falling asleep on me.

That won't be a problem, believe me.

Just be careful with my right hip, alright? I had it replaced last year.

I'll be gentle, I promise.

You'd be appalled at the things you accept about yourself the older you get. I had *accepted* the fact that I'd spend the rest of my days here in this home. *Alone.* I had *accepted* the fact that romance for me was nothing but a relic. A thing of the past.

I *accepted* the fact that I'd never fall in love again.

The loss of appetite was gradual at first. Not to mention the thinning hair. But all that weight loss, *good heavens.* The pounds were suddenly plummeting from my body. Thirty pounds in less than three months. I was so tired all the time. Lifting my arms above my head simply to slip out from my own clothes was enough of an ordeal to tucker me out altogether.

I had absolutely no idea what on earth was wrong with me. I figured I was just growing old.

Aren't we all, here?

I hadn't planned on getting a checkup—up until I saw Mr. Talbot chatting with Wendy Pendleton in the cafeteria. That was rather unscrupulous of him, if you ask me. Poor Wendy's Alzheimer's makes her such an easy target for sexual predators like Mr. Talbot, thinking he's her dead husband half the time. She may be able to forget his philandering, mere minutes after it's happened—but the rest of us have to watch their little charade play out, *day after day*, before he moves onto his next conquest. Cruising the cafeteria for yet another widow to conquer. Acting as if he's some septuagenarian satyr. And look how the rest of the gentlemen here have followed merrily along behind him, taking Mr. Talbot's lead. Passing around sexual partners as if we were all in some sort of free-for-all here. Mr. Talbot sleeps with Miss Pritchard, then Miss Pritchard sleeps with Mr. McClure, and then Mr. McClure sleeps with God only knows who, *and on and on and on*, passing along all kinds of venereal diseases amongst each other. First it was herpes. Then genital warts. Before long, it moved onto gonorrhea. Now the place is crawling with crabs! And yet, nobody says anything about their symptoms. Not to the nurses or to the doctor on call. Not to their children or even to each other. *Not a soul*. We've all been in denial about our STDs because we're ashamed or we're afraid *or we just don't know*. We have absolutely no idea what's happening to our own bodies because, good heavens, how could we? How could any of us have known about something like this?

I hopped on the B-17 bus, venturing downtown by myself to one of these free clinics you see advertised on the television so often. The nurse had no idea what to do with me—looking even more mortified than I was, I suspect.

Forgive me for having to ask this, Mrs. Temple, but . . . are you sexually active?

Possibly. If that's really any of your business.

Have you been engaging in unprotected sex lately?

What is there to protect myself from?

Now, Miss Temple—if you're having unprotected sex, I need to ask: Do you know if your partner has been tested for any sexually transmitted diseases?

That's quite enough. Thank you very much . . .

But Miss Temple—

Thank you for your time. Excuse me.

It's the parents who're supposed to preach the birds and bees to their children. Not the other way around. Certainly shouldn't have to give the speech to their grandparents. But it seems we may all need something of a refresher course here. *Sex ed for septuagenarians.* Schedule it on Wednesday, just before macramé.

Margery—it's your nana calling. I need your help, I'm afraid . . . It would appear that your grandmother has—well, your grandmother has caught some kind of bug and she. Well. She doesn't quite know how to handle herself. Could you call me back when you get a chance? And please—don't tell your mother. Thank you . . . Love you. Miss you.

My T cells seem to be holding up, I'm told. The nurse at the clinic encouraged me to contact all of my previous partners. Warn them of any potential infection.

That meant talking to Mr. Talbot one more time.

No cold shoulder today, hey, he harrumphed. *To what do I owe the honor?*

Nathaniel . . . I took in a deep breath. *There's something you need to know.*

That so? Well . . . ? What is it?

I was seventeen when I first met Walter. My family had rented a cottage along the beach, spending our summer by the ocean. I was walking along the shore one afternoon, wearing this soft red one-piece I'd bought just the day before. I looked over—only to find this boy sitting in sand, ogling me all over. His jaw dropped to his chest. *Where in the world did he come from?* I remember thinking to myself, looking at him from the corner of my eye. He was cute. Of course. Kept wondering if he'd say anything to me. Strike up a conversation to make me stop. Make me stay. If he was going to say something, he needed to say it now. Say it fast. Clock's ticking. Only a couple more steps before I'd pass, continuing on my merry way. His mouth must've opened a dozen different times. Only nothing came. *You left me speechless*, he told me much later. *I couldn't find the words.* I found that hard to believe. All I knew was, the longer he faltered, the more steps there were between us.

And just as I was about to disappear down the shore, walking on without him—I turned my head and said. And said—*Beautiful day, isn't it?*

Yes. Walter nodded. *Yes, it most certainly is.*

Remember how warm the water was, Walter? The two of us waltzed in together and just melted away . . .

cul-de-sac descending

A 29-year-old pedophile posed as a 12-year-old boy for two years and attended an Arizona school for four months . . . even convincing two men who had been looking for boys on the Internet that he was a minor and getting them to pretend to be his relatives.

—News.com, 2007

The family all felt it'd be best if Uncle Lonnie enrolled me in middle school once we made it here in Arizona.

My transcripts are looking pretty patchy from all the transferring by now. Three schools in four months. Uncle Lonnie even came to one of those parent-teacher nights, hoping to be as hands-on with my education as possible. Get a feel for the school. Meet all my teachers. But they say the same thing, no matter what state we move through: *Casey seems to keep to himself. Sits in the back of the classroom. A bit shy. Fairly quiet. Withdrawn.*

And the real clincher: *Looks as if he's been held back a couple times.*

I'm the perpetual seventh grader. Some grade school repeat offender. I've been held back enough by now, one look at me sitting amongst all the other students and you can just sense there's something different.

Not my fault. It's all because of puberty. Seventh grade's when everything changes. That final calm before the hormonal storm. Your voice drops an octave. Hair weeds its way up from every crevice. And acne, acne everywhere. Suddenly there's a scent to you that hadn't been there before, cold cuts warming up in the microwave, your brand-new body odor breaks out all over your skin.

Seventh graders can sense the shift in each other, like dogs sniffing each other's assholes. They can tell who's gone through puberty and who hasn't.

But there's always that one boy sitting at the back of the class, that one kid who's been held back a grade or two, always a little older than the rest.

His body's already changed.

All I'm trying to do is fit in. Let everyone see I'm no different.

Five feet eight inches. Not like I'm the tallest seventh grader around.

One hundred and twenty pounds. There are bigger boys in my class.

Arizona was supposed to be a clean slate for us. A fresh start for the whole family. First time in six months that our house wasn't on a set of wheels. We were in a subdivision now, complete with kids. Finally had a chance to make some friends. I'd set up a bike ramp in the center of our cul-de-sac, popping wheelies in the street. Looked like some peacock out there, flaunting its feathers in the road.

Took a couple weekends of playing by myself before some boys finally walked over, asking if they could ride with me.

Cul-de-sac. Even sounds like some kid's coin purse.

Befriending families during church services was easier than it should've been. A heck of a lot easier than in school.

Lock-ins are the best. The parishioners' children all corralled together. No escape until next morning. No parents. Nothing but all-night movies, board games galore. And pizza! The empty boxes still lying out, lids flung open. No one ever eats their crust, tossing them back into the box when they're done. Could've been bones, the remnants from the last slumber party strewn about the rec center floor.

My chin was feeling a bit bristly, so I brought my toiletry kit along with me.

I had figured a quick shave before leaving for the lock-in that night would've lasted me all the way through to the morning— but sure enough, one look in the bathroom mirror and I could see there was a shadow already spreading across my face. I double-checked just to make sure everyone was still sleeping before pulling out the razor. My shaving cream. A little foundation and a tube of liquid camouflage for the crow's feet.

Grandpa always tells me I have a baby face. Saying things like, *We've got to put that baby face to good use.* He helps me with homework, determined to make me maintain a C average. When we first met in a chat room in Montana, he had told me he was twenty years old—so when we planned our rendezvous in a hotel room off Route 32, I was a bit taken aback by the old man sitting at the edge of the bed, a shock of white hair reaching out from the side of his head. His sunken chest, collapsing with every labored breath. The shriveled nipples. Dried cranberries.

Family isn't always bound by blood. Hunger does just the same sometimes. And to be a member of our family, everyone's got responsibilities. Chores to do.

Mine's to make friends. Invite them home.

Grandpa always calls it trawling. *Drop your bait in and see what nibbles.* I have a couple weeks to make a friend before the family packs up and pushes on to the next town. The name of the game is to not draw any attention to myself. Blend in. That means waxing.

Never had a sleepover in Arizona before. You're the first. Which means you either wanted to be here—or you didn't. If you did—well, you know what that makes you. And if you didn't—everyone will believe you were, anyway. You know how boys are. Better to keep this sort of thing secret.

Between you and me.

Now that we trust each other, opening up like this—there's something I want to tell you. Something I've never told anyone before.

I'm not really twelve.

Take how old you are and multiply that by two. Then add the number of public schools I've enrolled in over the last four months. Then add the number of days it took them to catch on in Phoenix. Chino Valley. Then subtract the last number of years that I've been capable of charading as a minor with the aid of razors and makeup. Then add every member of my family that's in our house right now, cousins, uncles, grandparents, all of them just dying to meet you.

That'll be in the ballpark.

v.d.

Sheldon—I think it's time you and I had a talk. Could you spare a moment for your mother, please? I've dedicated the last seventeen years of my life to raising you, all I'm asking for is five simple minutes . . .

Three minutes.

Two.

I can help you get ready while we talk. Look at you. You can't leave the house looking like that. Your cummerbund is on all crooked. Let me at least fix your tie . . .

Hold still for me.

Now, I know this is something your father would want to talk to you about. He's better at this sort of thing than I am. But since he's out of town right now, it's up to me to discuss this with you.

There comes a point in a boy's life when he begins to change, Sheldon. Your voice begins to break. There'll be hair growing in places where there wasn't any before. Your skin's suddenly riddled with pimples. All these adjustments are normal, perfectly natural. Something every boy your age experiences.

Your body's simply saying . . . *You are about to become a man.*

My little boy's not so little anymore, is he? You've grown up so fast. Seems like only yesterday you were tossing rocks at Nancy Lamia. Now you're taking her to prom. You believed she had cooties as a kid. Which might not be so far from the truth, Sheldon. Don't disregard those adolescent instincts so soon, son. They're there for a reason, sweetie. Believe me. They just might end up saving your life one day. Because the older you get, the more your attitude toward girls will change. You might find yourself feeling curious over the opposite sex, which is fine. It's perfectly natural. I'm sure you've begun to feel differently around your friends already.

What a mother like me has to worry over, though, is that you be a *Thinking Man*. We don't want you jumping into something that doesn't make sense to you just yet, now, do we? Just because you're suddenly having these feelings for your female friends doesn't mean you need to act upon them. Because once you're in over your head, honey, it becomes *very* difficult to find your way back up to the surface.

Adults call cooties STDs, sweetie. They don't go away once you grow up. We just gave them a better name, that's all. A young man like yourself has to worry over sexually transmitted diseases, unwanted pregnancies—*or worse*. Much worse! You can't just go around copulating with just anybody these days, sticking your little *hoo-hoo* inside some strangers *ha-ha*. That's dangerous!

Now I know you're nervous about tonight, honey. I am too . . . It's not every night you have your senior prom. You want to mark the occasion. Make it special.

But Sheldon, *please*. Listen to me. Before you do anything you might regret for the rest of your life, there's something I need to share with you . . .

Hidden inside every vagina is a little snapping turtle, tucked up, way up above the vulva. It lives within the uterus, just waiting for some young boy like yourself to come sticking his little man inside its home. As soon as you've slipped far enough in, can you imagine what happens? Can you? That snapper peeks out from its shell and bites right through you. Nips your kipper clear off. Before you can even think about pulling out—*crack!*—it's too late. You've got no little man left.

I know you want to go up there. Every little boy does. But that's a habit you don't want to pick up just yet, Sheldon. It doesn't matter whether it's a finger or a thumb or *your own organ*—when you slip inside Nancy Lamia's vagina, you could lose your manhood in one bite. It may feel appealing at first, wriggling behind her hymen—but once you're butting up against that snapper, it'll treat your member like a marauding home-wrecker, thinking you're trying to move in. And these turtles are very territorial, honey. They don't appreciate houseguests, no matter whose uterus you're in. Even if Nancy spreads her legs for you on the first date (*the little harlot*), once that snapper chokes down your chances at ever giving me grandchildren, there's no getting your little man back ever again.

They don't grow back once they're gone, honey.

You'll be a eunuch for the rest of your life . . .

Just be a *Thinking Man*, Sheldon. That's all I ask. When prom's finally wound down and you're driving Nancy home, just remember what we talked about tonight.

Could you do that for your mother?

Please, sweetie?

You look so handsome, I think I'm going to cry.

My little boy's become a man.

Remember when you were younger? You were such a chronic nose-picker as a kid. I thought I'd never get you to stop sticking your finger up your nostril. I'd constantly catch you snorting your pointer up to the knuckle. The number of nosebleeds I had to mop up, I can hardly even count.

I remember trying to teach you to quit, insisting that you listen to me when I told you about that snail hiding inside your head. You thought I was joking. Up until the blood began to flow. Then you listened to your mother.

Now. Let me get a picture of you before you go.

sixteen again

... [O]ne procedure, known as hymenoplasty, is performed primar-
ily for the impression it will make on men. The surgery, which takes
about 30 minutes, restores the hymen, the membrane that typically
covers the vagina prior to first intercourse.

—*WASHINGTON POST*, 2007

The hymenoplasty was a present. For my husband. Our fifteen-year anniversary was right around the corner and I was dead set on giving him a gift he'd never forget. Something special. To mark the occasion.

I wanted to lose my virginity with him.

Again.

The first time was an absolute disaster. Just clumsy and utterly unmemorable. I would've done anything to take it back. Do it all over again. We'd been going steady all through our junior year, so for my sixteenth birthday, *sweet sixteen*, Steven and I agreed it was finally time to take our relationship to the *next level*.

Tonight would be the night.

That magical night.

My parents were out of town, so the house was all ours. I'd spent the whole afternoon getting my bedroom ready: scented candles scattered across the bookshelves. Rose petals spread along the bed. Soft jazz seeping out from the stereo. And when Steven walked in, he found me lying on my side, laced into this cobweb of a negligee I'd picked up at the mall earlier that afternoon. Just waiting for him.

Wow, he said. *You look awesome.*

Take me. I'm ready.

Uh, okay . . . Here we goooo.

The sex itself was pretty forgettable. I remember it hurting at first. I remember Steven fumbling above me. I remember his breath spreading over my neck, these warm gasps blasting off across my skin before he finally released all that pent-up oxygen within his chest with one last heavy exhale.

And then—nothing. That was it. It was all over before it had even started.

Sorry, he panted. *I'm sorry—*

It's okay.

I don't know what happened . . .

It's okay. Really.

After having Janice, our second child, I'd just about lost all the feeling down there. Two kids was enough for my vagina to call it quits on me. Tautness was all gone. No pleasure whatsoever. *Too much tissue damage,* my gynecologist explained. I'd just about given up on ever regaining any sensation down below, so . . .

No more fun for me.

Now Steven's starting to lose interest. Not that he would ever say such a thing. I can just tell. We've been having sex less and less lately—and whenever we do, his attention always seems to wander off. His mind is just elsewhere. Not on me. His eyes will glaze over, like he's lost in his thoughts, as if he has to concentrate on keeping his erection, imagining someone else, some other woman. *Some girl.* I can't stop thinking about her myself, to be completely honest. Whoever she is. Have I ever met her before? Is she someone we both know? A babysitter of ours? Or did he just make her up? Some imaginary friend-with-benefits? Here we are, in the middle of having sex, and I'm thinking about who my husband is thinking I am. Suddenly the two of us aren't concentrating on each other. We're both imagining the same other woman.

Him wanting to fuck her.

Me wanting to be her.

Would you be happier if I had breast implants?

Honey. Steven smiled. *You don't have to change a thing for me.*

What about a little tummy tuck?

I love you just the way you are . . .

I discovered the *Hustler* tucked under the cushions of our couch. Thank God the girls didn't find it. Steven would have to explain that one because I'm definitely not ready yet. The cover was all crumpled, but I could still see the girl smiling back at me. Her glossy face was all wrinkled with creases now, as if she wanted to mock me for my age. For being older.

Freshman coeds cum home for Christmas break! 'Tis the season for barely legal teens popping their cherries!

I sat myself down on the couch and started flipping through. I wanted to meet this girl from the cover. I wanted to have a talk with her. When I found *Shannon* on page fifteen, legs spread wide open so that I stumbled upon her vagina before I even saw her face—completely shaved, these airbrushed petals of pink budding up between her legs—I knew, *I knew* right then and there, this was the girl.

This was her. Steven's glossy little fuck-buddy, all tight and shiny.

I've been saving myself for the biggest cock I can find, says *Shannon* alongside her centerfold, the quote printed just next to her pussy. *I want to lose my virginity with somebody who'll make me beg for it . . .*

You'll beg, all right.

Beg to get it back. Beg for a second chance.

Because it's never going to be as magical as you believe it should be, Shannon. It'll be clumsy and awkward and painful and fast and forgettable and regrettable and all over before you even realize it's begun.

There's no do-over for a deflowering, Shannon. You will be robbed. Robbed of the one thing the world promised you. That supposedly made you so special.

They say your virginity is a gift you can only give away once. Once it's gone, there's no getting it back.

Turns out they're wrong.

My gynecologist promised me that revirginization is completely safe. More and more women my age are asking for vaginal rejuvenation than ever before. I wasn't alone.

The hymenoplasty only cost me three thousand dollars. He performed the procedure right there in his office. He put me under a local anesthetic, numbing the area while he restored my hymen, surgically reattaching the torn tissue until it was perfectly intact again. He rebuilt the membrane as if the last twenty years had never happened. All sealed up and ready to go in less than thirty minutes.

Surgically, I'm a virgin again.

I'm pure once more.

I went to the mall and picked up a pair of the sexiest underwear I could find to hold my new designer vagina. A couple weeks from now, after I'd healed, Steven would unwrap my panties and find his anniversary gift waiting for him.

Perky. Practically *Playboy*ed.

This was for both of us. This was the best anniversary present a husband could ever get. He could deflower me all over again.

I'd been giddy about it all week, acting like a little girl.

Because I was. A part of me was.

Down there.

I had stranded myself on my own little nubile island, hidden in the middle of an ocean of childbirths, these ripples of stretch-marked flesh lapping at its pert shores. The rest of me may have looked the same—but down here, on this island, *my island*—I was young again. *New.* A Robinson Crusoe of the cunt! You better believe I was never coming back.

I was sixteen again. Sweet sixteen for a second time around.

We'd sent the kids over to a friends for the night. The house was all ours. I'd spent the whole day cleaning, picking up all the different dolls left on the floor, sneaking a peak at their Plasticine pelvises.

Our evening started off with a candlelit dinner. A bottle of wine.

Now it was time to exchange gifts.

Ready to open up your present?

Oh, honey—you know you didn't have to get me anything . . .

If you want it, you'll have to follow me.

Where to?

. . . The bedroom.

I'd planned everything perfectly. Rose petals. Scented candles. Soft jazz.

And my hymen. My brand-new, recently restructured vagina—complete with enhanced vaginal muscle tone.

An entirely resculpted vulvar structure, all for him.

Is that . . . ? Steve started to ask.

Yes.

How—? How did you . . . ?

Happy anniversary, baby, I whispered into his ear, pulling him in as I leaned back onto the bed.

When he first inserted himself, he tore through my hymen like a little boy ripping into his Christmas gift. All greedy. No regard for the wrapping paper whatsoever. Simply giddy for the gift inside. There was pain. Pain I hadn't felt in years. I couldn't tell if it was the surgery still needing to heal or not. This—this felt different. This felt tender. This ached, all raw and throbbing.

This was my first time all over again.

The two of us were suddenly acting like teenagers, fumbling over each other. I watched as Steven navigated his way through my tight confinements. This was all new to him now. He was dealing with unfamiliar dimensions for the first time in years, nervous and excited all at once. I saw the pleasure spread across his face.

He kept his eyes open, on me. No closing them now. No need to retreat off into his imagination. To *Shannon.*

Staring straight into Steven's eyes, I clamped my Kegels down and held on tight. I embraced the pain. I reveled in it. I let out a cry of joy with each thrust.

First stroke:

Yes! This is exactly what I had paid for.

Second stroke:

Yes! This was my night. Finally my magical night.

Third stroke:

Yes—

Steven's eyes rolled up into his skull, eyelids fluttering fast. His lips pulled back into a grimace—and in that moment I understood, I understood what was happening. Steven was slipping. Steven was losing control. Steven was coming inside me already—*Oh oh God oh God oh God ooooooh goddamn it!*

The gift was gone again. My gift. It was over before it had even started.

Sorry, he said. *I'm sorry—*

It's okay.

I don't know what came over me.

It's okay. Really.

The next morning, when I woke up, I saw there was blood on the bedsheets. Red speckles spotting the cotton.

COMMENCEMENT

part one:
staph infection

Sarah Havermeyer, *forty-one*

They gave me my own waiting room. Hid me in the pediatric wing,
far away from the other families. It's much quieter at this end of
the hospital. Less hectic here. Less parents, less press. I spent the
last hour simply listening to the hum of fluorescents over my head.
Went over to the window on a whim once, lured in by the camera
flashes. The parking lot's all gone now. It's suddenly engulfed in
a forest of transmission antennas, budding up from the roofs of
these news vans. The network call letters look like initials of young
couples carved into the bark of each tree:

KBCW-TV plus WGBO-4.

WDBJ-7 hearts WSLS-10 4-eva . . .

When Mitchell was much younger, he and a handful of kids
from the neighborhood all went out into the woods behind our
houses to play a game of hide-and-seek. When it was Mitchell's
turn to be *it*, he leaned his head against his own tree just as everyone else had before him. Closed his eyes and counted to a hundred. By the time he turned back around, he found himself facing
the woods all alone.

Ready or not, here I come—echoing through the trees.

But what Mitchell didn't realize—and why would he, really—was that everybody else had already run home by then.

Didn't stop him from playing, though. Peeking behind each tree. Searching for his friends.

An hour went by before I was on the phone with the neighbors, asking if they knew where Mitchell was. But none of their kids would say, shrugging their shoulders.

When there weren't any parents left to call, I took to the woods myself. Flashlight in hand. Finally found him leaning against a tree, huddled into himself. *Shivering.* Poor thing caught pneumonia that night. Had to take him to the hospital, waiting in this same room.

Want to tell me what happened?

No.

We can keep it between you and me, if you'd like. Promise I won't tell.

I don't want to talk about it.

There are never any magazines here. Nothing but coloring books flung across the floor. Crayons scattered all around, like shell casings discharged from a rifle. Every color of the rainbow falling to the floor, round after round after round . . .

Not that I feel like reading right now. Simply had that reflex to flip through something. Get my mind off things. Picked up a coloring book without even realizing what it was at first, skimming the pictures just to pass the time. Glancing at all the empty animals, empty cartoon characters. Page after page. Their blank bodies filled in with scribbles. No consideration for coloring in the lines, whatsoever. You'd think they'd all been shot, every animal hemor-rhaging Crayola across the page, their splatter pattern in Razzle Dazzle Rose or Tickle Me Pink.

The number of times I've sat here over the years, waiting amongst all the other mothers—I've lost count by now. They blend together after a while. All the checkups. The mumps. Flu shots. Chicken pox. Not to mention ear infections. A tonsillectomy. A sprained wrist. The list just goes on and on . . .

It's a wonder my son even reached high school.

How any of our children made it this far.

Not that the news is saying anything. Not until the police notify the next of kin. The reporters have been recycling the same infor-mation for hours now, the live coverage sounding stale already.

No names yet.

Just numbers.

Last time I had to wait this long, it was because Mitchell had swallowed something he shouldn't have. *Marbles.* Started com-plaining about his tummy aching at the dinner table, refusing to finish his macaroni—so the very next day, I brought him in for an X-ray. And sure enough, there they were: a constellation of bright white contrasting against that ghastly black of his stomach. The negative image of a half dozen glass pellets settled into his belly. A grape cluster tethered together in pale veins.

Benjamin Pendleton had put him up to it. Said he'd be his *best friend* if he swallowed the whole set, all ten marbles. And to think that Mitchell had almost made it, more than halfway there. He was determined to earn Benjamin Pendleton's approval, to win this po-sition as his pal, *bestest friends,* only giving up once his throat constricted itself, his own esophagus refusing to swallow anymore, no matter how hard he tried, no matter how hard he forced himself to eat one more, *just one more*, begging with his own throat to let him ingest just one last marble before stumbling back home, sick to his stomach.

To *prove* his worth. As a *friend* to Benjamin.

Want to tell me who put you up to this?

No . . .

Mitchell. You're only hurting yourself by not saying anything.

I don't want to talk about it!

The police have been ushering all the parents in through the rear entrance of the hospital, away from the camera crews. The second I saw Wendy Pendleton in the hallway, barely able to even stand on her own two feet—I knew why she was here. Recognized her right away, even though we hadn't spoken to each other in ages. Not since our sons were in the third grade together. Her eyes had glazed over. Nothing but a pair of marbles settled into each socket, flickering under the fluorescents. Felt like I was staring at a teddy bear. Not some mother who'd just identified her son.

They've placed a police officer right outside my door. *For my protection,* they say. They're worried some wandering father might find me here, hiding amongst the stuffed animals. The jigsaw puzzles. The coloring books with the mottled corners, their pages sticking together from all the constant gnawing. Seems as if children choose to chew through these books rather than read them. The edges are still wet, even after office hours have come and gone for the day. The pulp rubs right off between my fingers. I'm thinking of the poor puzzle with its missing pieces, all of them dissolving inside some sick kid's stomach. Nurses have to sanitize these toys at the end of every day, spraying them down with disinfectant. They have to kill off the bacteria before the following morning. Before it starts up all over again. One child will pass along their germs to whoever puts the same stuffed animal's filthy limb into their mouth next and they'll end up catching something completely different than whatever it was that they walked in here with.

Seems fitting to be sitting here, then. Almost like old times. Wouldn't be so surprised if a nurse were to walk in any minute now, calling out Mitchell's name—*The doctor will see you now.*

But none of the nurses will even come near me now. Won't look me in the eye. As I passed them all in the hallway, they simply bowed their heads. Focused on the linoleum rather than face me. As if they were afraid? *Of me?*

The press is about to take my boy away from me. This is my last chance to have him all to myself, the way I want to remember him. Before I have to give him up.

Let him go.

I'm imagining some reporter sifting through the yearbook, flipping from page to page, just to find his photograph. Before long, Mitchell's face will be broadcast all over the news—which is unfortunate, since he never took his class pictures seriously. He'd never tell me what day they were being taken, so I couldn't force him to dress up. Look nice for his picture. By the time I'd find out, it was always too late. They would've already snapped off the shot. If I ever wanted to order any photos for the rest of the family, I'd have to buy these wallet-size prints of him in one of his ratty T-shirts. His hair all tousled. Refusing to smile for the camera.

Can't even bring myself to look at his yearbook now. Seeing him there, surrounded by the rest. Their faces clumped together, grinning all around him.

Nothing but an obituary now—the whole yearbook.

This grim assembly of smiles.

The world will weep for the children of Midlothian High—but no one will weep for mine. I'll have to cry for my child alone.

You won't find his name amongst the others. He's been omitted from the list of victims. Not that he was ever invited into their club anyways. Mitchell was never asked to play with the rest. They'll say it was my son who took their children away—but what none of these parents are willing to admit is that their sons and daughters took my child away from me long before today. Mitchell had the bruises to prove it. Half our trips to the hospital were for fractures that magically happened on their own. Sprained wrists that mysteriously appeared out of nowhere, no explanation whatsoever. Black eyes that looked like black holes, swallowing up my son, the distance deepening within his gaze.

Every time, *every time* I've had to sit here in this room, I've lost a little bit more of my son. It was only a matter of time before there was nothing left of him to take back home.

Can we talk?

. . . Why?

Want to tell me what's been on your mind lately?

No.

Anything happening at school?

No.

What about—

Mom.

Can't we just chat? Just for a minute?

There's nothing to talk about.

There's plenty.

Just let it go, Mom.

Please, honey . . .

I said no! Just drop it.

All I want is to sit with the rest of the parents.

I want to wait amongst the other mothers. To mourn with them. I've lost my child, too. Why can't I sit with them?

We deserve to wait together.

Found a stray puzzle piece at my feet, softened with some child's saliva. There's no telling what the picture's of. Has a fleshy complexion. Even feels like flesh, the cardboard all soaked in spit. Its interlocking tabs are so flimsy, they'll flap back and forth whenever I rub my fingers over them.

Came across another piece tucked just behind the leg of my chair. Same color, same wet texture. The two pieces fit together perfectly.

Suddenly the picture's coming into view.

Here's a piece of his cheek. A tooth. A shard of his skull, a clump of his hair matted with blood. Fragments of his face, the skin still adhered to the bone.

I'm picking up what's left of him off the floor. Hundreds of tessellated flecks of flesh and bone, blown apart at close range. I'm passing the time working on this jigsaw puzzle of my son's face, just to get one last look at him.

High muzzle velocity.

When Mitchell was done, he slipped the gun over his tongue. The blast reached through the roof of his mouth. Ruptured all the soft tissue before bursting through the back of his skull, sending puzzle pieces all over the classroom wall.

Kids will put anything into their mouths.

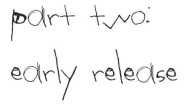

part two:
early release

Julie Keady, *seventeen*

Give me a name. Any name.

Pick any student from this school and I bet you I can list off all the books they've ever checked out without even needing to use the computer.

It's a talent I have.

Got a lot of time on my hands here. Besides, it's more fun to flip to the back of the book, to the index card holstered along the cover. All the students who've ever checked it out are right there—a winding column of names in different colored inks, different handwriting. Dates winding backward. Some so far back, well before I had ever set foot in this school, the names don't even sound real anymore. Like ghosts.

Mitchell's name pops up in a lot of library books. More than most students here. Sometimes his name is the only one listed, written five times, each on top of the other. Ten times. Filling up the whole card.

Do Androids Dream of Electric Sheep? October 15th to November 2nd.

Slaughterhouse-Five. January 10th to the 23rd.

A Clockwork Orange. February 13th to March 6th.

One Flew Over the Cuckoo's Nest. Page 86. In the margins, in different colors of ink, you can read—*So what'd you think?*

What?

The book. Did you like it?

The movie was better.

You should totally check out Animal Farm. *It's about communism but with pigs.*

I started eating lunch in the library as early as my freshman year. Spent my study halls there already, shelving books for extra credit. I'd always been a bookworm at heart, no matter what my friends said. They'd tease me about it all the time—but I was itching for Ivy League, so I needed my transcripts to prove it.

One of my jobs here was to flip through the books. Find the vandalism. White out the dirty doodles. Erase all the explicit scribbles. That sort of thing.

Mitchell would take notes. He circled words. Phrases were underlined. Particular passages were boxed in with pencil. I felt guilty for having to rub out his thoughts. I'd read over all his annotations before erasing them, seeing if I could figure out what he thought about the book. Whether or not he liked it.

Nobody else checked out the books he did. Not in a long time.

Breakfast of Champions. Page 45. In the margins, in different handwriting, you can read—*Since you've already departed from the required reading list, you should totally read* Naked Lunch *next.*

What's that?

William S. Burroughs. We're not allowed to carry it here—but I've got a copy at home, if you're interested. I could let you borrow it. I'll leave it on the third bookshelf, second aisle. Between Whitman and Wordsworth.

Whatever.

Students will say they each had a moment. An encounter with Mitchell that they never mentioned before. Never brought up. Not until now, when everyone's looking. At the time, they'll say, it didn't seem like such a big deal. But now—*now*—if they'd only told a teacher, maybe, just maybe, things would be different today. Maybe they could've stopped this all from happening. They want to say they saw the warning signs. They want to lay claim to've known all along.

Truth is—none of them ever cared. Mitchell Havermeyer was a social ghost, haunting the hallways of this school long before he shot himself.

Students will never let him go. He's all ours now.

Our own bogeyman mascot.

Mitchell would sit by himself in the library, always with some book open before him. His mom still packed his lunch. Always the same sandwich—PB&J. A Granny Smith and a ziplock full of Oreos. Four Oreos. A can of soda with a napkin wrapped around it, soaking up the condensation so that it clung to the can. And on the napkin—a note from his mom, written in Magic Marker. The words were all blurred, the letters loosened by the wetness, ink bleeding into the napkin.

Brave New World. Page 132. In the margins, half in cursive, the other half in print, you can read—*Have you read* Lord of the Flies *yet? Think you'd like it.*

How do you know? You don't know anything about me.

This was totally against library policy, I know. The librarians would've kicked me out if I'd gotten caught. But I had an idea. Since Mitchell checked out the same books more than once, as soon as he'd return them and I'd have to attend to my requisite scribble rinsing—I'd find his notes in the margins and try responding with some of my own. *Pen pals.* It'd be fun. It'd all be there, everything we ever wrote. Our correspondence was tucked away in the pages, where no one would find us.

No one would ever know.

Establishing contact had to begin broadly. I had to cast a wide net, responding to four or five of his favorites. It was impossible to tell which book he'd choose to check out next. I had to look at his patterns, trying to determine what he'd want to read all over again.

1984 or *The Dharma Bums. Catcher in the Rye* or *I Am Legend.*

First contact was in *On the Road*, page 33—*What's up?*

Simple. Straightforward. Nothing too complicated. I wrote it right below a bunch of his notes before slipping the books back on the shelves. Didn't sign my name or anything, keeping it anonymous.

Two weeks later, his response—*Who's this?*

I wrote back—*Did you know Kerouac wrote this book on an endless sheet of paper?*

Two weeks later—*So what?*

I wrote back—*He didn't want to waste time switching out sheets, so he fed a whole roll into his typewriter. That way he could just keep writing and writing and never stop. Pretty cool, huh?*

Two weeks later—*Sorta.*

A chain of exchanges started to stretch down the margins, each link in different ink. Took a month to fill up a single page—but it was working.

We were talking.

Sort of talking.

In *Neuromancer* I wrote—*Did you know William Gibson came up with the Internet before anyone else had even thought of it?*

Two weeks later—*Really?*

I wrote—*Cyberspace was totally his idea.*

Two weeks later—*That's pretty cool.*

I could pop up in any book at any time. He'd never see me coming—but once I was there, we'd deface the pages together, filling up the margins for entire chapters. Whenever we would exhaust the blank boundaries of one book, we'd move on to another.

See you in Fear and Loathing in Las Vegas, *page 86 . . .*

Catch you in The Plague, *chapter three . . .*

Find me in Nova Express, *page 23 . . .*

We would run out of books at the rate we were writing now, burning through the whole library before the end of the school year.

Where do we go from here?

How about a bigger book? Like Dostoevsky or something? That way we'll have some space . . .

Okay.

Crime and Punishment, *page 42.*

We never said anything to each other outside of our correspondence. Passing him in the halls, I acted as if I didn't know him. Nobody did. None of my friends, nobody. Our lives outside of our messages didn't matter. It didn't matter who we were here. Who was popular and who wasn't. We had created a space completely independent of high school politics. In these books, we were free to be whoever we really were.

Nothing else mattered.

A Confederacy of Dunces. Page 312. In the margins, in interlacing handwriting, weaving together like a braid of hair, you can read—

Who are you?

Don't you know? A friend.

What makes you think I'm your friend?

Because only ghosts can see other ghosts.

I wanted him to know that I saw him. That no matter how shitty the kids at this school treated him, he wasn't alone.

We wrote each other for all the fall, through the whole winter. We'd kept our correspondence secret for nearly the whole school year.

Then I was asked to give a speech for our graduation. Still shelved books for extra credit during study hall, but suddenly I was spending less time in the library—using my lunch period to work on what I was going to say to the rest of the school. Everyone kept asking me—*What're you gonna write? What're you gonna write? What're you gonna write?*—over and over again, like a broken record.

Everybody but Mitchell.

He was supposed to return a book to the library the day of the shooting. When study hall came and went and he hadn't brought it back, I wondered where he could be. Usually he returned his books on time. He'd had the book out for the full two weeks. It'd be overdue by the end of school and he'd be fined ten cents for each day he didn't bring the book back to me.

I'd been sitting in history, working on my graduation speech when I heard a pop outside. We all heard it. The whole class. Could've been band practice. The drum corps must've been rehearsing in the hallway, the rapid fire of a snare rattling through the rest of the school. But the rhythm felt awkward. The tempo was off. There was a quick succession of bursts. Then nothing. Again—one beat, two. Silence.

Then we heard screaming.

Mitchell walked right into room 202. This wasn't his class. For a second, I thought he must've found out that I was his pen pal—barging in like he'd been looking for me all day, wanting to let me know he'd finally figured it out.

Kim Young-Lee had been sitting beside me. I watched her flop over onto her desk, as if she'd fallen asleep all of a sudden. Carl Santoro was sitting on the other side. His body slithered out from his desk, slumping to the floor. Jamie Temple used to sit with me on the school bus when we were in kindergarten—and here he was, one row back, right behind me, taking a bullet directly in his chest.

There was a pop. Then another. Felt this pressure against my chest.

I looked up at Mitchell and realized—

He didn't recognize me.

The shelves have felt emptier since the shooting. The tally is two dozen books by my count, long overdue. The students who checked them out are all dead now.

How's the library supposed to get those books back?

Third aisle. Second shelf from the top. Fifteen books in. Between Emily Brontë and William Cullen Bryant. You'll find the last book Mitchell ever checked out. His last act as a student here at Midlothian High School was to return his library book. It's been reshelved, back in the stacks.

No one's checked it out since. No one probably ever will again.

Robert Browning. *The Pied Piper of Hamelin.* The title circled. It's his pen. Same ink. Particular passages underlined. Complete stanzas cordoned off.

Flip to page 18. In the margin, in Mitchell's handwriting, you can read Mitchell's last correspondence—*Where'd you go?*

He never realized I was his pen pal. Now he'll never know. No one will.

This is where I live now.

This is my home.

part three:
keynote speaker

Mary Keady, *forty-seven*

Julie was supposed to deliver this year's commencement speech. She'd agonized over it for weeks. Fretted over every sentence, wanting each word to be perfect. I'd peek into her room whenever I'd see her lights were still on late at night, finding her fast asleep at her desk. Her cheek resting on what she'd written thus far. Took every bit of willpower I could muster not to read it, peering over her shoulder.

You're gonna have to wait until graduation, Mom, she'd say, catching me red-handed. *You'll hear it along with everybody else.*

Julie always sat in the front of her class, no matter what the subject. She always tried to be as close to the chalkboard as humanly possible. Never wanted another student's head blocking her view.

She took three bullets—all by herself. The entrance wounds lined up along her chest, like a row of red ribbons, the rosettes bursting through her shirt, as if she'd fallen short of taking home first prize at this year's science fair.

Second place second place second place . . .

Graduation was sparse this year. Less in attendance, less parents. Half the families who'd lost their children didn't even show.

The Pendletons. The O'Rourkes. The Connors.

I went.

My husband had been against going but I made him attend anyways. I wanted to hear this year's keynote speaker. I wanted someone to make sense of what had happened—and who better, really? I wanted to hear what their advice would be for the future. What words of wisdom they'd dole out to the students who survived.

Aim high. Achieve your dreams. Don't give up.

They got our governor to step in at the last minute. To ease our school's collective pain. He spoke of healing. He spoke of forgiveness.

But he didn't speak to me.

Brought along my camera. Didn't seem right to go to graduation without it. I listened as each student was called up, one at a time. Their names echoed throughout the auditorium, the loudspeakers making them sound hollow.

When they finally reached the *K*'s, I pulled out my camera, ready to snap off a shot, listening to the assistant principal run through Kagan, Kagebeck, Kahn.

Julie Keady . . .

She'll rise up from the mass of gowns and tassels, taking the stage.

Julie Keady . . .

She'll step up to the principal and shake his hand, receiving her diploma with the other.

Julie Keady . . .

She'll turn toward the audience, facing every parent sitting in that auditorium. Waving her certificate in the air. And I will be right there, clicking off the picture. Saving that moment forever.

Julie . . .

They skipped her name. Hopped right on to Anne Kellaway and kept going.

Lancaster.

Lassiter.

Lee.

I listened to her slip farther and farther away from me.

Manuella.

Matthews.

Ming.

Why wouldn't they let her graduate?

I'd been weeding our garden when the phone rang. I figured the answering machine would pick it up, so I didn't budge. Just kept on digging. But as soon as the machine would click on, the person on the other end would hang up and call back. Had to've been a salesman soliciting for something. *Are you happy with your current phone service provider?* Who else would keep calling like that? Over and over again . . . You'd think they'd leave a message if it was so important. Here I am, on my hands and knees. All covered in dirt. Certainly wasn't about to track mud all over the kitchen floor just to answer the phone.

That's why I was the last parent to the hospital.

Bill had beaten me to it. The police had called him from work. He'd already identified Julie's body by the time I got there, sitting amongst all the other parents in the waiting room. No need to identify her again.

But the police weren't going to let me see. They told me I was too late. If I wanted to see Julie for myself, I'd have to wait.

Wait for what? I asked. *What else is there?*

We buried her the day after graduation. More parents showed up to the memorial service than to their own kids' commencement, forced to swap ceremonies at the last moment. For those families that had lost their children, rather than watch them graduate, we all attended each other's funerals.

I saw the Pendletons. The O'Rourkes. The Connors.

No Sarah Havermeyer.

Her son wasn't amongst ours. Mitchell's yearbook picture wasn't one of the dozen framed photographs wrapped in their own floral wreaths, standing upright at the front for all to see. I turned around at one point during the service, sifting through all the students and teachers. Just to see if I could find her. See if she'd show up. Pay her respects.

Julie's principal took the podium, directly addressing all the parents. He spoke to us of healing. He spoke of forgiveness.

He didn't speak to me.

The police returned Julie's backpack after they'd rummaged through it. Her commencement speech was inside. Tucked into her French textbook. I couldn't bring myself to read it. Only a few days before, there was nothing in this world that I wanted more. *Nothing in this world.* I tried. Several times, I held the paper up to my face, making it as far as the first sentence before the back of my throat began to burn.

Her words deserved to be heard. They needed to be read out loud. Because letters of acceptance keep coming in, even now. All the scholarship offers. The study guides. Because colleges keep sending Julie housing surveys to figure out which dorm she'll be living in next year.

Because she never got to read it herself.

Because she never got to stand up at that podium and share her words with the rest of her friends, ushering the graduating class into the real world.

Because I was robbed of watching her walk.

Because we deserved commencement.

Because I'm fed up with the empty rhetoric. All these speeches, these promises of pushing on.

Because of her son.

Because of her son.

My daughter finally graduated today.

Sarah Havermeyer was the keynote speaker. She didn't answer the door right away. I could sense her on the other side the door, leaning into the peephole. There was no need to ring the bell again but I went ahead and did it anyway, acting as if I didn't realize she was standing there, staring back at me.

Mary? She kept the chain lock between us.

Sarah. Can we talk?

I don't know, Mary. My lawyer said I shouldn't . . .

Please—just let me in.

The ceremony was simple. Just the two of us, together. Alone in her house. In her living room. The front door shut, sealing us inside. The ticking of a clock from another room. Pictures of him, of Mitchell as a kid, nothing but a little boy, framed on the wall. Watching over us.

And Julie's speech—that single sheet of notebook paper, folded and refolded over a dozen different times.

We called out their names. We called up the graduating class. Sean Connor. Paul Hastings. Kim Young-Lee. Robert Marasco. Benjamin Pendleton. Tammy O'Rourke. Carl Santoro. Jamie Temple. We watched them rise up from the mass of gowns. Their tassels continuing to grow. God help me—I saw worms. Like a million wriggling diplomas—I couldn't stop myself from seeing them. Flinging their hats high, the air above our heads eclipsed in graduation caps—their edges as sharp as shovel blades, breaking open the earth and burying their bodies.

Read it.

Please, Mary . . . Please don't make me do this.

Read the speech. Now.

Sarah brought the paper up to her face, sobbing. The page was only inches away from her mouth, getting wet. The words were distorting, unleashing their ink.

What is graduation? Some say it's the end of the best years of our lives. Now that we're about to enter into the real world, there's one big question that's lingering within all of our minds—What happens next?

Hearing her speech, quivering out from Sarah Havermeyer's mouth, all I could do was close my eyes and listen. Let the words take me away.

And for a moment, for just a brief moment—I could hear her again.

Her words came alive.

And in that moment—I'd never felt so proud of my daughter in all my life.

My baby girl finally graduated.

Most graduation speeches talk about how close we've become as a class. But ten years from now—we won't be chanting Go Trojans! or Senior power! We'll be remembering the friendships we made, the relationships we shared. For once, we all look the same. Blue gowns. Tassels on top of our hats. But even though we look alike in this very moment, it's our differences that make us who we are. I believe each one of us here has the potential to become something special. To become someone. To make something out of our lives and change the world as we know it.

So back to that big question—What happens next?

I say the answer is:

Anything we want.

LOVE
STORIES

Fillings

Had someone's pacemaker pop in my ear today. Lost about half of my hearing on the left just because this windbag forgot her husband had an artificial heart. Could've been a grenade going off. That's how loud they sound when they explode. Thirty minutes in, this guy's battery starts to melt, all those combustible chemicals flaring up below his rib cage. His chest just detonated. The blast blew the door right off the retort, peeling my eardrums away.

Nearly went deaf in a heartbeat.

In a heartbeat.

That's why there's this form the family has to fill out for the deceased, acquainting us with all their implants. Hip joints, dental work. We want to know up front about the stuff that doesn't burn, because—once you're cremated, all that's ever left are the things that held you together while you were still alive.

Screws and pins. The rest just gets swept away.

There'll be some bone fragments, sure. Usually a chunk of the lower jaw. Maybe the upper bulb of a femur. But depending on the departed, I'll find a filling buried below the ash. Somebody's bridgework shimmers out from under all that gray. Polish it off and it looks just like a gold nugget.

As a kid, did you ever take a field trip to one of those rock quarries? Remember sifting for semiprecious stones with your science class? Your teacher gives you this grate, some wooden frame with a wire mesh stapled over it. You pan for malachite and amethyst all day, like some miner during the gold rush. You dump a shovelful of mud into your sieve, straining away all that sand and sediment, until that one gem rises up from the muck. A little chunk of fool's gold glimmering under the sun.

The great thing about my job is that I'm sifting for fillings as if I was in the fifth grade all over again.

Dental gold holds up under intense heat. Dentists have come up with these casting alloys—adding platinum for its durability, palladium for its malleability, copper for its biocompatibility. Even zinc.

These inlays were built to last.

They end up outlasting you.

Can't think of a better testament to our love than that. *Till death do us part* takes on a completely deeper meaning.

Think about it, honey. A gold cast crown usually weighs in at eighteen karats. That's three-quarters pure gold! Step in to any of these jewelry shops and they'll tell you the same thing. White gold is simply a mixture of other metals. Platinum, palladium, copper. Even zinc. They'll say they've cut their engagement rings with the exact same alloys you've got holding your fillings in.

And you deserve something that's going to last. I want a ring that's going to say, *My love for you is so strong that it can withstand the test of time, holding up at two thousand degrees Fahrenheit.*

Because all I ever see is what gets left behind. Our bodies are consumed with heat and flame, reduced to nothing but ash and swept up into some cooling pan. Our bone particles are processed by a machine, ground down to the same consistency for the urn. All that's left of ourselves are the artificial limbs and false teeth. The hip replacements and fillings. The metal residue of our negative space, occupying whatever cavity we had, whatever emptiness we needed filled.

That's what your love does for me.

You are my filling, honey. You make me feel complete.

Which is why I had this whipped up . . .

Eighteen karats. Solid white gold. It only took five fillings! From their mouths to mine, we're all asking the same question . . .

Will you marry me?

overbite

Before we go any further, honey, I've got to warn you . . .

I've bitten off the tongues of more men than I'd like to remember.

All by accident, now. Don't get me wrong. I've left men speechless all across this country.

You simply take that risk when you kiss a lady like me. My mouth might as well be a roulette wheel—the moment it opens, you're gambling your taste buds away. The muscles along my jaw limber up the longer we make out, until your tongue tickles the roof of my mouth—and then, *crack*, my mandibles snap, sealing my teeth together like a bear trap.

They call me the Iron Jaw for a reason, sweetie. Once my masseter muscles cinch, there's no unlocking them. I can hang from that harness for hours, spinning by my teeth until I've nearly chewed through the trapeze. These pearly whites have held me in the air for half my life, allowing me to spend as much of my time suspended above the audience as I have on the ground.

I was born into this business, see. My mother and father had worked me into their act by the time I was five, raising me in the air. Once my baby teeth had all fallen out, they started feeding me carrots for every meal. Just making me masticate my day away, until I'd laced my jaw in a thick strip of sinew. I had the puffiest cheeks you'd ever seen. My buccinator muscles were bulked beyond belief. Adults always *ooh* and *ah* at me, thinking I'm cuter than a little Kewpie doll. None of them know I'd bitten off about half of my own tongue before I'd even turned ten, snipping another millimeter off in my sleep almost every night. I've been left with a lisp, mincing my words like I'm talking with my mouth full all the time—that scab at the tip of my clumsy tongue tripping me up on my pronunciation. People think I'm mute, sounding all deaf and dumb—so I just keep my lips sealed, talking to nobody.

I've been bound to the big top by my jaw for years.

I've wanted to leave. Tried a hundred times. No matter where we perform, there'll be *men* lining up by my dressing room door, all of them promising to take me away from all this. But I've chewed through suitors like a box of chocolates, nibbling into enough men to know what's really at their center. Those promises always end up empty. Their intentions are never as sweet as they seem, believe me. Most of them just want to cop a feel, slip me a kiss when their wives aren't looking.

But then I met Reginald.

He'd been waiting for me at my dressing room, standing by the door. As soon as I come walking in, he's handing me a bouquet of roses, saying he's never laid eyes on a beautiful thing like me. He'd seen the show once already, sitting in the front row the night before. The second he saw me hanging from that harness, he said his heart started palpitating like a popcorn kernel about to burst.

He'd come back on his own the very next night, just to see my routine all over again. To see me. Our show was running for the week, the tent set up along the outskirts of this town, giving him a chance to see me wriggle through the air for the next five days straight. And he kept coming back, night after night—waiting for me once each show was over, another dozen roses in his hand. My trailer was littered in bouquets by the end of the week. I could barely get to my bed, there were so many.

Once we crossed the state line, I figured that would be the last I'd see of the man. But in the middle of my routine the very next night, I looked down into the crowd . . . and found Reginald sitting right there in the front row, marveling up at me. He smiled, which got me to grin back—only for my lips to slip. I almost lost my hold of the trapeze. The audience gave a gasp as I nibbled my grip back onto the bar—while Reginald just stood up, opening his arms, ready to catch me if I was to fall.

Nobody had ever wanted to be my safety net before.

Reginald was waiting for me after the show as always. No roses this time, though. He had a wedding ring. *Twenty-four karats!* He was willing to leave everything for me, he said, as long as I was willing to leave the circus. He promised me a house. I'd have a home that wasn't on wheels, never needing to hit the road again. I'd be rooted for once. I didn't know what to say. My jaw just— dropped. Empty of any words.

Reginald rushed up and kissed me, pressing his lips against mine. My mouth only opened wider, his tongue easing inside. He tasted like liquor, as if he'd slipped a sip of whiskey into his system before seeing me, helping him work up the courage to propose to me. I'd never drunk any alcohol before. My tongue suddenly stung with its aftertaste. My eyes started to water, that liquor burn was so unbearable. There was a tap at my gag reflex, as if some rat had just stepped onto a mousetrap—setting my jaw right off. It simply swung shut, my canines clamping together. Everything within my mouth went warm, this sudden rush of blood swelling up inside my cheeks. And his tongue was still flickering over mine, as if Reginald wanted to keep kissing me. It wriggled down my throat like some determined worm, aiming for the heart of this apple. Choking, I didn't have much choice but to swallow. This twitching bit of muscle made its way down into my stomach. I could feel it quiver through, settling into my belly.

Reginald fell to the floor, his cheeks just streaming red. Whenever he tried to scream, his lips would split to a flood of blood—gurgling up a wet sound, bubbling out from his hollow mouth.

I swore to myself that I'd never let something like that ever happen again.

I kept clear of my male admirers. I denied their company after every show, no matter how adamant they were about seeing me. I refused to talk to anybody, keeping my lips sealed for weeks. I only opened my mouth for the trapeze.

With my lips wrapped around that handle, hiding these teeth, I've dangled over these men's heads like I was bait.

I'm the circus's worm.

I hang off this fishing hook, luring these men away from their money. If any of them are brave enough to bite, making their way backstage, they won't even realize they've been snagged. Not until I have to unhook them. Not until their lips are pressed firmly against mine and my reflexes kick in, uprooting their voices for good.

I've got a dozen tongues tumbling around my tummy right now. I've digested the ejaculations of the most eloquent men, living off of their prattle and false promises, as if their chatter had all the nutrients I needed to survive, while the circus eats the rest.

Did you see me up there tonight?

The audience was speechless, getting all tongue-tied through my routine. Halfway through the act, I wondered what it'd be like to let go. Just open my mouth and drop. I bit down on that handle so hard, it nearly snapped in half. When an animal's caught in a snare, it'll chew through its own leg to set itself free. Me—I'll just have to gnaw my way through this harness. Free-fall through fifty feet of air.

You'd catch me, wouldn't you?

Of course you would. You wouldn't let me down.

Come on now, honey. Don't be afraid.

Kiss me.

Just a peck. I promise I won't bite.

birdfeeder

Wasn't until winter when word finally got around about Michael. A group of hunters discovered his body about three miles into the woods. First day of deer hunting season usually brings back a month's worth of venison stretched along the front hood of every Chevrolet in town—only this year, most trucks came back bare, their empty fenders still caked with a crust of dried blood from last season's kill.

Looked that way, at least. Maybe it was just rust.

Instead of heading to Sally's Tavern, where everyone parks their cars to compare their quarry, see who won the citation, who brought back the biggest buck, sneaking their beers out into the parking lot even though they know it's against the law, Sally turning a blind eye to her customers as they buy their beer and duck out the door again—this afternoon, first day of deer hunting season—most men just rushed right over to Sheriff Flaherty's office on their own, as sober as a bunch of newborn babies, leading him and a handful of his officers up Route 2, right where the highway lines up alongside the woods, nothing but miles and miles' worth of trees, parking their trucks in the ditch next to the road and cutting through the forest.

Heading right to Michael.

They say it was John Whalthorne who found him. He'd been following this buck for about a half mile, keeping his distance until he knew he had a clear shot—his eyes wandering through the woods by way of the scope attached to his rifle—only to catch some color in his crosshairs. This flash of blue.

Turns out to be Michael's Levi's.

The weather had washed the brightness out. Months' worth of rain rinsed the dye away. His favorite pair of pants had faded into this phantom hue. This baby, baby blue.

His bones were nothing but wind chimes now, knocking up against each other in the breeze. Birds had begun to take him away, one peck at a time, plucking what pieces of him they could pull free with their beaks, bit by bit. He looked like a bird feeder up there, hanging from that branch.

Everyone knows the woods are where you go when you want to keep a secret. The deeper into these trees you reach, the darker the secret you want to keep.

The only secrets I've ever kept are about Michael.

He'd lay a leaf against my chest, watching it rise and fall with every breath—the frond mimicking my rib cage, only smaller, as if it were two chests pressed against each other. His breath always tasted of cigarettes, like dried leaves at the back of his mouth. My father always thought the two of us were sneaking off into the woods to have ourselves a smoke, smelling cigarettes on my breath every time I'd come home. The funny thing was, I never had a cigarette in all of my life.

Only Michael.

We'd make our way out to this clearing in the trees, taking the entire day just to walk there—hiking further and further into the forest, until there was nothing around us. Nothing at all. Not the hum of a truck, not the whir of some lawn mower. Not another human being for miles. We'd lie on our backs, slipping out of our T-shirts, feeling what sun could make its way through the trees. These specks of light rested on our chests. That's where I'd kiss him. I'd let every patch of light lead my lips across his body, as if the sun were saying—*Hey, kiss him here.*

And—*Kiss him there.*

Thinking about Michael out there, all winter. Hanging by that branch, the tension in his neck relenting more and more. Thinking about his body breaking down, changing colors. Shifting pigments. Thinking about all those birds swooping down, pecking at his neck. Tugging on his lips as if they were earthworms. Taking away what they could carry back to their babies, dangling his lips over their beaks.

It wouldn't have been far off for people to believe Michael had run away. He'd done it a couple times already. Only difference is he'd always come home. Whether it was a few hours or a day on the road, Michael would always make his way home. So when it reached a week, his mother started to worry. Like *really* worry. But by then Michael was already in the woods, slowly disappearing, trying to hide himself inside the stomachs of every animal willing to nibble on him.

Thinking—*Nobody would ever look for me in here.*

Thinking—*It's safer inside these stomachs.*

The weather and elements had decimated the rest of his clothes, chewing through his T-shirt until it was nothing but scraps of fabric. You couldn't even recognize the Metallica decal ironed along the front. The *E* and the *T* were just about the only letters left. The rest had peeled free, flaking off into the air.

I was there when he bought that shirt, wearing it to school the very next day. I remember how firm it felt when it was new, like cardboard, the cotton starting off all stiff, the creases in its sleeves keeping crisp for weeks, before finally feeling it descend into its tenderness. He loved that shirt. He would pull it off and place it under my head, as a pillow. The two of us rested on the ground, looking up at the sky just above us, a few stars hanging over our heads. The trees blocked out the rest, braided in by branches, as if I'd put both of my hands right over my face, this latticework of fingers hiding the sky from my eyes.

We spend the night out in the woods, telling our parents we were sleeping over at each other's house. Holding him, I remember listening to the trees warping over our heads. Every bending branch made this squealing sound in the dark, until it almost sounded like my arms were bending as well, the weight of Michael in my grip causing my limbs to twist.

What if someone finds out about us? What do we do then?

Don't worry, he said. *We're safe out here.*

He was wearing those blue jeans the last time I saw him, nearly six months ago now. Pretty much wore those pants every day of his life, anyhow, but I know it was when we were together last, when I last laid eyes on him, that I was the last person to see him alive.

Because there was no note. No cry for help.

Just his body, breaking down.

People keep asking me why. *Why would he head out into the woods alone and hang himself, waiting out there all winter for someone to find him?* Suddenly I'm an authority on his unhappiness? I'm the expert on what makes him tick? Even Michael's mother comes to me, desperate for some sense of closure, just so she won't have to blame herself for what happened. *You were his best friend, Sean. He would've talked to you about these things. Did he ever mention depression? Did he ever say anything about suicide?*

I knew he was out there.

When Michael first disappeared, I went out into the woods by myself—going to the only place where I felt safe, where I could be alone.

And that's when I saw him. Swaying. His head bowed against his chest.

It was better for someone else to find him.

Someone other than me.

If I'd been the one to take Sheriff Flaherty out into the woods, *other* questions would get asked. Questions like—*What were you doing out there in the first place?*

What were you two boys doing so far out in the forest, alone?

Questions like that don't stop themselves from getting asked, even if you provide an answer. In a town as small as this, sometimes the answer isn't what people are after. Sometimes they want your secrets.

That's what frightened Michael more than anything. That's what sent him out into the woods by himself. Sometimes, saying your lips are sealed isn't enough. The best way to keep a secret?

Cinch your throat shut, cutting off the air that cushions your deepest, darkest truths.

Deer hunting season would come in a few months. Someone would stumble upon him. They'd rush back for Sheriff Flaherty, dragging him through the woods and cutting Michael's body down. Doing it properly.

Until then, I'd know where I could find him.

I'd know where he'd be.

I've kept him secret for months now, never mentioning Michael to anyone. Because there are more secrets where that came from. More than I can count.

I keep his eyes, as blue as his jeans. I keep his lips, as thin as earthworms. I keep the taste of his mouth out in those woods.

Nobody knows about him and me out here.

president of the fan club

The girls all got together this weekend to discuss our fundraising efforts over poker. Adele, our treasurer, said we've made a little over two hundred dollars in our first month alone—which puts us ahead of our estimated goal of five hundred dollars before February. Adele believes we'll have raised enough money to buy all five of us a bus ticket to Aberdeen by the end of the month. To speed things along a little bit, I proposed we all pick up the pace with our bake sale. Instead of just a dozen cookies, we should each make two, selling them for twice the price we normally would. If this was just to raise more money for our children's drama club, we wouldn't even dream of charging ten dollars for our Hershey's Kiss cookies. Most of the time we just buy the batch ourselves, figuring the money's going to a good cause.

But this is bigger than band boosters. You're more important than new uniforms for the football team, Wallace.

I've been saving this evening dress I wore when me and my husband first met. I'm going to wear it to the penitentiary, just for you. It's a few sizes too small for me to fit in anymore—but we girls have all regimented ourselves, devising a diet that we swore we'd stick with. *No white sugar, no white flour!* I won't even lick the spatula after mixing up a batch of cookies.

My husband doesn't know why I'm trying to trim my hips. He thinks it's for him. Which is fine. If our spouses want to believe we're all burning off the pounds for their sake, they won't worry over our road trip. None of them will ever wonder why we decided to head down to Aberdeen instead of Daytona or Las Vegas. And the less questions we have to answer, the better.

We're keeping you to ourselves, Wallace.

We're not sharing you with anybody.

The girls normally meet at my house for our poker nights. I'll ask my daughter Shelby to do her homework in her room. She's too young to understand what us girls are up to. It's better for her to believe we're excited over the idea of getting away from our families, our housecleaning, our grocery runs.

You never make me feel like a housewife, Wallace. You've never made me clean up after you. Never asked me to shave the hair off the back of your neck.

When I imagine that we're in bed together—the second I switch off the light, you're always on top of me, rubbing your hands all over my body, wrapping them around my throat. You dig your thumbs under my lower jaw, your palm pressing down on my Adam's apple. You stare me right in the eye until I start to feel light-headed.

After clipping all your newspaper articles, I imagine I'm one of those women you met along Highway 45. It took us girls a long time to decide who got to be who. Adele was determined to be Nancy Tucket, going head-to-head with Luann. The only thing that was so special about Nancy Tucket was that she was the first body the police found. That doesn't mean she was your first, though—which is why I didn't want her, myself. I had my heart set on Cheryl Lynn Simmons, the girl you picked up in Meridian. You just dumped her body in some ditch. The girls and I have argued over why. Adele thinks it's because the cops were close by. You were running out of time. Me, personally—I'd like to think it's because you saw something in her that struck your fancy. She was too beautiful for you to ruin like the rest.

I could've been Cheryl Lynn Simmons.

I look at that Glamour Shots picture of her they printed in the newspaper—and I swear, there isn't much difference between us. I dyed my hair to look just like hers. I'm a brunette, now. Your favorite.

Don't tell the girls I did this, but I dipped into my bake sale funds to pay for a makeover. I figured it was a business expense, so they wouldn't mind. I went over to the Glamour Shots and got me the same deal Cheryl Lynn did. I brought my copy of the newspaper along to show them her photo, explaining exactly what I wanted. For days, I practiced that pose, making sure I tilted my chin just the way Cheryl Lynn did. Her smile was the hardest part. Her lips are sharper than mine. I couldn't get my mouth to make the right angle. My grin looks a little lopsided. But other than that, you can't tell the two of us apart.

You be the judge. Tell me what you think. I included a copy of my picture, just for you to put up on your wall.

So Adele gets to pretend she's Nancy Tucket, while Luann settled for Polly Portent. Naomi took Charlene Reynolds while . . . I'm Cheryl Lynn!

We all feel like we're different women now. Walking outside, I feel like anything is possible. You could be just behind a bush, waiting for me to step away from the porch light—then you grab me from behind, putting your hand over my mouth so I won't scream, dragging me back where nobody can see us.

I had to wait a while before I could write you tonight, holding out for my husband to fall asleep. It took him a while to doze off—leaving me lying there in bed, staring at the ceiling. All I could think about was you. How you make me tremble just from imagining you near me. You make me feel alive, Wallace. Every time you made the news, my heart would stop. Our lives were in danger because of you. Women all throughout the county were asked to stay inside, keep away from the highways at night. But for us girls, we started making trips to the supermarket at eleven o'clock, right after the news anchor finished reporting on another body found along the highway. After we knew where you'd dumped her on the interstate, we'd figure out where the nearest grocery store was— meeting up in the dairy aisle fifteen minutes later. If one of us girls didn't show up, we'd know why. We'd all be envious of her. I'd drive home slowly, hoping you'd still be out there on the road, looking for a ride—your thumb sticking out, your smile so wide.

The judge will just have to understand, it can't be considered manslaughter if the victim's willing. In your defense, our home life will be all the evidence you need.

Take me away from my life, Wallace. I'm ready for you.

oldsmobile

A couple in their eighties who left their east Texas home two weeks ago for a 15-mile road trip were found dead in their car, hidden by dense brush more than 350 miles in Arkansas. Lela and Raymond Howard apparently became disoriented.

—ASSOCIATED PRESS, 1997

The wind? The wind hasn't been in our hair like this in years.

Couldn't even tell you the last time we had the roof pulled down, ushering the air in from all around. The current's uprooted every pin holding Lela's hair in place. Her curls are spilling over her shoulders, all steely and gray, this burst of silver blossoming around her head.

God bless you, Doctor Charles McDuffy. You discovered the *medial superior temporal area* just behind my wife's ear, pinpointing that little bit of brain tissue that provides the mental map for her to comprehend where she is and just how she got there. If it weren't for you, she'd be sitting in our living room right now, wondering where in the world she was, her mind losing its grip on our own home, gradually decaying away with the days right there on our couch.

It's because of your breakthrough that we're even on this road trip. Since her sense of direction has completely deteriorated, where she's been, where she is, and where she's going are all gone now. Her internal compass has lost its ability to help her navigate anywhere anymore. Our very own neighborhood is a maze she can't escape from. Just the other day, Lela tried to drive herself to the grocery store. She hopped in the car and pulled out of our driveway, turning right rather than left. Drove four blocks before she completely lost track of where she was, tangled up in the latticework of streets and cul-de-sacs.

Wasn't until that evening, almost seven hours later, when I received a phone call from a neighbor, ten blocks over, telling me Lela was wandering about their backyard garden. She thought she was in the produce section, sifting through the greens for the best head of lettuce.

Are these still on sale? she asked, holding out a coupon clipped from the morning's newspaper. *Two for one, yes?*

You called it motion blindness. *The patient has lost her capacity for path integration,* you said, flashing your little penlight into my wife's eyes. *I'd strongly advise you not to allow her to get behind the wheel of her car anymore.*

But you never mentioned anything about my maroon 1960 Oldsmobile Super 88 convertible.

Three-hundred-ninety-four-cubic-inch V-8 engine. Three hundred fifteen horsepower. This baby's able to move all four thousand pounds without as much as even a whimper from under her hood. The odometer is nearly up to ninety thousand miles—but the faster me and Lela drive, the lower those numbers go, winding backward with every mile forward, taking the two of us through decades' worth of highway that we haven't traveled down in ages.

Alzheimer's has given me my wife back.

She's twenty-three years old today. We're on our honeymoon all over again, heading west along Interstate 40. The rattle of tin cans tied to the rear bumper trails in our wake, clattering across the asphalt. There's a bed-and-breakfast waiting for us in the California panhandle, only fifty-five years away. We'll reach it within a few bends of the cerebellum. Until then, it's just Lela and me and the open road. The wind's ironing out the wrinkles in her face, leaving her looking as young as the day when we first took this trip. She's leaning against the headrest, her neck bent back. Just taking in the sun. With her hair whipping around, it looks as if she's still wearing her wedding veil—this wave of ivory washing over her face. She wouldn't take it off, insisting she wear that veil clear across the whole country.

Better be careful, I warned her. *You don't want to lose that.*

It's not going anywhere.

We'd made it as far as Albuquerque before it finally blew off. Lela flipped around in her seat to catch it, watching it drift away without her.

Told you so, I said. *Now there's no getting it back.*

But that hasn't stopped her from trying. Lela keeps reaching for the clouds just above her head, grabbing at the air. She'll bring her hand back down, all balled up into a fist—releasing her fingers slowly, expecting to find a slip of satin inside.

I'll get you yet, she keeps repeating to herself. *You just wait.*

Our children will probably be wondering where we are before

too much longer. By the time they call the authorities—my wife? She will be seventeen. The two of us will be on our first date again, where I parked the car at the top of Macarthur Park, one of the highest points in our hometown, overlooking the cityscape, the entire skyline spread out before us. My hand will make its way from the parking brake across the upholstery, reaching for her knee—while I try to keep as calm as possible about it, clearing my throat as I lean over for a kiss.

Take that hand back, mister, she'll say, her eyes never breaking away from the windshield. *If you want to keep your fingers, then keep them to yourself.*

She won't let me kiss her for another three years!

Ever since my stroke, the right side of my body has remained partially paralyzed. Makes it difficult for me to reach that far over anymore. Lela has to lift my arm up if we want to hold each other, wrapping it around her shoulder.

With one hand on the steering wheel and the other around my wife, we're cruising through the years and we're not looking back.

There's no telling where we are anymore. There's no knowing how far we've gone. The odometer says we've only driven three hundred miles—but ever since my wife's dementia settled in, we're seeing parts of our past as far back as our trip to the hospital, when Lela gave birth to our daughter, to day trips to the beach with the family, even holiday jaunts across the country, visiting distant relatives.

Lela looks over at me—and she doesn't see the elderly man who has taken the place of her husband. She sees me? At thirty-three.

She sees me at eighteen. She sees me wherever her memory wants to take her.

All I'm doing . . . ? All I'm doing is escorting her there.

The windshield's thick with insects now. What's left of their wings flickers in the wind. The number of bugs smashed against the glass is beginning to eclipse our field of vision, just like the amyloid plaques and tangles clustering up within Lela's brain, blotting out her ability to remember the names of our own children.

Which is probably a good thing.

It was our daughter who first suggested that we should consider assisted living. *There's no way the two of you are going to be able to take care of each other anymore, Dad,* she said. *Not with Mom's memory fading as fast as it is. We need to start thinking about the future.*

We're fugitives now.

We are on the lam from our own family. All we've got is the highway, an expanding canvas stretching ahead of us.

How old we really are? Doesn't matter anymore. It's all new to her now. We're on a never-ending road trip, where every bend brings back another memory of who she was.

We can't stop now.

If I can just keep her in the car, driving her Alzheimer's in circles, then I can keep Lela from forgetting where we first fell in love.

Did we just pass your parents' house?

Think we did.

Can we pull over? I haven't visited with your mother in ages.

We have a full tank of gas. The radio's turned on and the volume's up as high as it'll go. The windows are all rolled down. The wind is everywhere.

This road is ours.

the interstate and on

If there was ever going to be a time when it'd come down to the cross
or Taylor's class ring, I know he'd fight for prom. When they'd take
our picture, he'd want to be the one around my neck and that close
to what counts. That's the way he put it, talking about my heart.

Felt good having two men scramble over who got to be mine just
for some picture, especially since one of them was God. For Taylor
to step up to the Lord like that, I knew it had to be important. I figured I could at least give him the night. I switched one for the other
on a silver chain from my mom's jewelry case, thinking I could handle it. It'd make him happy.

When I first saw Taylor buttoned down in that suit, I could tell as
easily as I'm telling you he didn't feel right inside it. I figure if you're
going to put a man in something that proper you'll lose a piece of
him, just how your little brother hushes up once he's in his Sunday
clothes. Taylor was either getting buried or standing at the altar.
Which one I couldn't guess just yet.

There was this second, maybe two, where the living room held itself just the way it was for a while. It got me all quiet for some reason
I don't think I can explain.

Dad was asking for a photo before we left. I made sure I had everything facing the lens, that my sides weren't showing too much. I held Taylor's hand over my stomach, just to be sure.

It's funny how the pictures you take in your head stay a lot longer when there's no noise around. I'm thinking about pinning the flower on his jacket, his hair combed out of his face. He's just standing there in front of me in his tux and all I want is for him to see his ring. I want to show him where he is.

You should have seen his car ahead of all that. He'd filled up the tank. He'd even gone through the wash to get the hood shining. I could see the color of my dress on its side before I even reached the door. My face didn't show. Arms weren't there, either. All there was on that metal was this purple stretched over the car.

The roof had been peeled back and the windows were rolled down. That's something he hadn't done in a while. I waited for Taylor to open the door for me. You expect those kinds of things when you're talking about prom. I'm thinking about him waiting to see if I've got all my dress in before he shuts the door, how he's going to look at me before heading over to his side. He hadn't said much of anything about my dress yet.

There was a bottle of something at my feet. It had that half-empty sound to it, which made sense. I kept it in between my shoes, the neck held under one heel, my dress covering it up. Taylor's behind the wheel, not moving or anything. His hands are dead on his legs. He's pushed himself as far into the seat as it'd take him, his head over on one shoulder. The keys aren't even in the ignition yet.

I want to talk about it, he says to the wheel. He leaves it at that for a while, giving it time.

This was gonna be my first prom.

Senior year and I'd never gone to a dance before in my life. We had to vote on a theme at the beginning of the year. Everyone I knew picked A Night Under the Stars. The juniors spent the day cutting out decorations from cardboard. Tickets had to be bought the week before at ten dollars a pop. Fifteen for couples. When you paid, they signed your name and your date's name on the ticket and then on a list of all the people coming. I had been third in line, putting us at the top of the list, which meant when people would give their names, they'd have to pass by ours every time.

It had taken me a month to get my dress ready. I wanted the time to show in each stitch. Stores can't give you the feeling of a homemade dress just as much as they can't give you someone to wear it. I did it all myself, and he'd know it.

We're out on the interstate and the wind's lifting up my hair, tossing it in my face. There's a whistle in my ear, but I can't see where it's coming from.

He was only giving me half of his face. The other half he wasted on the road. When he'd look at me, I knew he was listening because his eyes wouldn't flinch the whole time I was talking. Not many people will even give you that much. Parents won't listen and friends are always thinking about something else. It's guys like Taylor who'll give you almost anything just to hear you talk.

The streetlights are slipping away. All the other cars are disappearing. I'm counting the divider lines rushing by. I'm seeing the dashboard through the bottle and it feels like I can swallow each of those lights down, sipping one gauge after the other. My mother had yelled it into me that once you start getting that weight inside, everything around you starts changing. *Your insides are just the beginning,* was what she'd said. *People's faces stretch open as much as your belly does, voices sag just as your breasts do.*

My seat belt's working down my dress. That strap's feeling around my stomach. It starts to rub over my sides, searching for something. The whole car starts feeling different to me. The door's getting soft under my hands. The upholstery's getting wet. Gravel's spitting up from under the tires, hitting the belly of the car. Doesn't make for much but I've got listen to it anyways. Both times I reached for the radio, there's Taylor's hand turning it off.

I'm halfway through the liquor he's left behind. I offer him some, bits of my hair sneaking into my mouth. The wind's in everything and I can't manage to say what I want to say, my throat's tickling so much. It comes laughing out of me and I spill some of the bottle on my dress, the color going deeper. I watch it spread over my knee.

Taylor's just looking to the road. He's got the panel lights on his face, making his cheeks all green to me, his eyes holding onto something out there. I wait for the blinker to say we're turning. I don't think I've ever put so much faith into a turn signal before. The overpass comes into the headlights and he's not letting up on the gas. I'm thinking he's teasing me. So I hit him in the shoulder, trying to tease him back. I keep it up when we head right past the exit, laughing at him, giving his shoulder my fist over and over.

But he's not saying anything. He's not even turning his head to notice. The arrow picking up the miles per hour keeps leaning over, closer to me, pointing at me as if I'd done something. My corsage tightens around my wrist, cutting off my circulation, numbing the hand that's holding the bottle. Probably a good thing, at this point.

He swallows something back when I ask him where we're going. I follow the apple of his throat as it bobs down and rises up again. His neck's getting red around his collar. I could see it getting sore from that far away. When I ask him where we're going, it takes a while for anything to come out of his mouth—and when something does, it's not coming from him. He says, *Let's go just a little longer, just a little farther down.* But I can't see his eyes right then, so I don't know who he's saying it to.

My dress is sticking to my leg. Every time I lift it up, it's like peeling away the top of my skin. My hands smell of alcohol. It's all down my leg. Wringing my dress out the way you would a dishrag. Wrinkles up the front. I don't know where the bottle's gone. I don't know where we are anymore. The exits are coming up one on the other and we're not stopping for any of them. Taylor's watching the road like there's something out there to find, something where the headlights stretch or even past that, but I can't see it. I'm asking him where we're going, getting nothing. I can see his chest rise, his tux pushing up against his seat belt. My eyes aren't holding on tight enough to focus on his face anymore. I can't help thinking in yearbook photos, looking at his hands on the wheel and picturing them around me. I imagine the whistling from around the car coming out of his mouth, into my ear. I'm still picturing us together at A Night Under the Stars. The clock on the radio says it's past the hour and I know there's a dance going on out there, somewhere, all these people coming in underneath tinfoil and streamers. The only decorations I can see come from the divider lines passing me by. The only lights I have are in the car, telling me how fast we're going, telling me what station I can't listen to.

Taylor starts telling the road everything. I picture myself picking up all the things he says and putting them in my belly, holding them there. He'd peeled the roof back for me, he'd rolled the windows down. And now he's telling the road that he can't handle me having it, that he can't handle everyone knowing.

I could show you photos of him from the seventh grade on, but I couldn't tell you what he looked like sitting right next to me. He was ten years old in one shadow, eighty in the next. You get these pictures in your head that you can't put down. I can see snapshots of us together out on the interstate now, holding each other's hands. My corsage is squeezing my wrist blue, his flower's pinned through his heart. I know I can see it now, all the things out the windshield. I'm thinking I can see what's at the edge of those headlights, and I wonder if Taylor's been watching the whole time.

I hear what the road's saying. *Something's gonna come out of the sky and save this girl, something's finally gonna get her to prom.*

I let my seat belt free. The strap whips me under the chin. My dress jumps up from my sides. Air touches me everywhere. I can feel the car pushing me forward, pushing me on. I think it wants me to get up. I grab on to the windshield and pull myself out of the seat. With my heels still on and everything, I stand up on the cushion and look out to the road from above the car.

Everything's on me now. I'm feeling the air from all over. Wind's whistling in my ears, slipping its way down my lungs. I can see where the road stops and the sky starts, and above that there's all the night you could picture.

You got me, honey? I ask, but I can't hear him. *Where are we going?* I ask anyways, just to watch his lips move for me. *Where are you taking me?*

I pinch my mouth shut and let the car go. I let go and hold my sides, holding onto everything inside. The headlights start grabbing for the ditches, their attention running off the road. My balance goes along with it and I start to slip. I get the wind from all around, closing my eyes and wrapping me up. It starts to raise me. It catches me by the dress and lifts me up. I lose the seat. There's nothing there anymore. I can't feel anything below me but all this wind. I can hear the wheels give a little of themselves to the road, shedding over the pavement, the sound of babies crying to each other. But there's nothing my feet want to touch, so I just hold onto myself and rise up into the sky. I'm spinning, dancing through it.

They said my jaw had been the first thing to hit pavement, kissing the road, breaking it in five separate places. Now it hurts to kiss anything.

The nurses told me a lot of things when I felt like listening. How luck saved me. *A miracle.* The hands of God lifted me out from the car not a moment too soon.

And then something about Taylor. Little things here and there, like his car running off the road, his body pushing through the windshield. Nurses say those kinds of things when they think you're sleeping.

It's hard to figure out where he is right now. Thing's aren't as heavy for me anymore. There's a scratch along my neck that came from his ring. That's what I like to think it is, anyways. It's better than gravel. Better than just some piece of glass. I picture it out on the interstate still, next to some of him, some of me, left with all the other things they couldn't pick up.

the battle of belle isle

They dumped Benny by the river. She was wearing nothing but a green paper gown. Ambulance must've pulled over, rear doors fanning open. Bet the driver didn't even step out to help her. Just kept the engine running when they left Benny by the side of the road, all disoriented, shivering from the cold. No clothes, no shoes, no idea where she was anymore. Started making her way toward the water, all sixty-three years of herself crawling down the craggy rocks. Bare feet slipping over the algae. Rested just next to the James for Lord knows how long. All numb now.

There'd been rain out west, so it wasn't long before the river swelled. Couple of hours later and the surface rose right up to her, the currents whisking her away. Carrying her downstream for half a mile. Two miles. Maybe more—I don't know. Depends on where they ditched her in the first place, doesn't it? Can't shake this image of her floating over the rocks, half naked, whisked off into the whitewater. The rapids dragged her body along before bringing her back to Belle Isle.

This island had been our home.

After they shut down the Freedom House on Hull Street, you

either had to migrate up to Monroe Park or toward the Lee Bridge. The nearest mission now was nestled into this neglected valley on the south side of Chesterfield County, about a mile's walk out from the city limits. It had been home to some old battlefield long forgotten by now. Perfect for a skirmish during the Civil War— not much else. Only neighbors now were a couple dilapidated factories, the soil all soaked with arsenic. Just about the only thing you could build on top of that poisoned property was a homeless shelter. And this mission—their doors didn't open unless it was below thirty-five degrees. Come 6 a.m., you were woken up and tossed right back into the street no matter how cold it was. Locked their doors until the thermometer reached the right temperature again.

Me and Benny tried our hand at it for a couple nights. We hefted everything we owned back and forth over the Lee Bridge, just looking for work. Got all of our belongings on our backs. Must've looked like a couple of ragged privates marching with fifty pounds of provisions slung over our shoulders. Just praying for the mercury to sink below thirty-five. That one degree's the difference between you and your own cot, a cup of watered-down coffee—or freezing to death on some park bench.

Can't call that home. Nobody should.

Richmond's calling all this shifting around "revitalization"—but I'm not buying it. Pushing us out to the periphery. Forcing us to find a new home every night.

Their Downtown Plan has nothing to do with me.

Never had Benny's better interests in mind, that's for sure. When I first met her, couple years back, the boys in blue had just busted her lip for sleeping out in Monroe Park. She shuffled her way into Freedom House after curfew, an icicle of her own blood hanging off her chin. Weren't that many cots left at that hour. She took the one next to mine. Dropped her plastic bags, all her junk spilling over the floor. I leaned over, thinking I'd lend a hand, getting a slap on the wrist for my troubles.

Don't touch my stuff.

Just trying to help . . .

Help yourself is more like it.

Asked her what her name was. Her jaw refused to move all on account of the cold, so when she answered—*Bethany*—I didn't hear the *tha* part. Her tongue missed the middle syllable, like the needle on a record player skipping over a groove.

Sounded like she said *Benny.*

No funny stuff now, she said, brandishing her wrinkled finger like it was a blade. *I'll have you know I'm a respectable lady.*

There's gotta be thirty years between us! The hell are you expecting me to do?

Just better watch it, young man. I've got my eye on you.

Most folks made their way to Monroe Park after Freedom House closed its doors—but that was a trap, if you're asking me. Used to be a training camp for Confederate soldiers. Military hospital after that. Lot of cadets ended up dying on that patch of land. Too many homeless ghosts out there now. People who spend the night out there end up disappearing. Some say this city gives you a bus ticket to any town you want, one way, no questions asked. Just hop on board and *bon voyage.* But I'm betting that's just a rumor the boys in blue spread around town so you drop your guard and follow the brass right into the paddy wagon. Act like some mutt trusting the dogcatcher—transfixed by the biscuit in one hand, not even paying attention to the net in the other.

Benny's vote was to move to Monroe. Mouthing off about the handouts down there. College kids managed some meal plan for the homeless in the heart of the park. Serving up soup on Sundays or something.

Step in there, Benny, I warned her, *and you won't be walking out ever again.*

You're just being paranoid.

Sure shut down Freedom House fast enough, didn't they? Sure don't see the Salvation Army marching into Monroe to save the day. I'm telling you, Benny, the police own that park!

Then where the hell are we gonna go?

That left Belle Isle.

You got the Lee Bridge reaching right over the James River. Just another memorial to another dead Confederate general. Connects the south side of the city to the rest, shore to shore, like a stitch suturing a wound. The James River bleeds up from that gash, no matter how many bridges sew up this city.

But nestled in between the concrete legs of Robert E. Lee, there are about fifty-four acres of public park, all wrapped in water. The river splits, rushing down either side of the isle. Its converging currents form a sharp point at the tip.

A real diamond of an island.

Only way to reach land is to hoof it. Got this footbridge slung under the interstate, a little baby bridge suspended from its father. You can hear the hum of automobiles passing along the highway just above your head—but down there, once you've set foot on the island, it's like the city doesn't exist anymore. Sound of cars just melts away.

We'd be like—like our own Swiss Family Robinson down here.

More like Robinson Crusoe, Benny said, shaking her head.

No one'll bother us, I promise. As long as we stay on the far side of the island, away from the footpaths, no one'll even know we're here.

You're crazy, you know that?

No more missions, no more shelters, I said. *We'll never have to set foot on the mainland again.*

Yeah, yeah . . . Just lead the way, Friday.

There are the ruins of an old hydroelectric plant tucked away on the far side of the island. Closed its doors in '63. The electric company gutted out all the iron, leaving the concrete behind. Nothing but a husk now, all empty. Good for a roof over your head when it gets raining. We set up camp in one of the old water turbine rooms. Have to crawl through this hatch just to get in. The air's damp down there. Soaks into your bones if you're not bundled up enough. But the walls keep the cold wind from nipping your nose. Made that room a hell of a lot better than sleeping in some refrigerator box. The generator was long gone, the rotors removed, leaving behind this empty shaft as big as any room in these mansions you see lined up along Plantation Row. We're talking ballroom here. Perfect fit for all of Benny's stuff. She hefted a whole landfill's worth of accumulated junk with her. A dozen plastic bags busting at the seams, full of photographs. Toys. Anything she could get her hands on.

Home sweet home, Benny said. She started decorating the place right away. Slipped her pictures inside a rusted wicket gate like it was some sort of mantelpiece. All the shorn cylinders were full of photographs now. Every severed duct was a shelf for her past.

Who's that? I asked, pointing to this one black-and-white snapshot. Cute little brunette smiling for the camera. *She looks familiar.*

Who do you think?

You're telling me that's you? Didn't recognize you under all that baby fat.

Yeah, well—they fed me better back then.

The island's supposed to be vacant once the sun sets. Every day, like clockwork, this ranger comes to lock up the footbridge. Not like that ever kept the kids away. Teenagers always snuck in after dark, building bonfires. Spray-painting the walls. We had a whole novel's worth of graffiti wrapped around the place. Couldn't really read what it said. The words were barely there anymore, losing their shape. Tattoos fading into your skin. Reminds you of different times. Times when those tattoos would've meant something.

An eagle, a globe and an anchor.

Semper fi.

Nothing but blue lines now, wrapping around your arms like ivy overtaking a statue.

First time Benny saw the ink on my forearm, we were trying to keep each other warm while those teenagers broke beer bottles against the other side of our living room wall. Had to keep quiet. Just holding each other. That's when she noticed the lower fluke of the anchor, all fuzzy now, diving down deep into my skin. Gave her something to trace her finger along. I watched her run her pinkie over the lower hemisphere of the globe.

Bet it's cold there right about now, she said, pointing to where Antarctica would've been on my arm. *Colder than here, for sure.*

We were in the thick of December by then, the temperature dropping off into the low thirties. It was only going to get colder the deeper into winter we went. That meant less visitors. Less dog-walkers. Less joggers. Less families. Less of everything.

You know this used to be a prison camp?

Sure feels like one.

During the Civil War, I whispered. *Over five hundred thousand Yankee soldiers, right here. Couple thousand at a time, freezing their asses off in the open air.*

You're lying.

It's true . . .

The more we talked, the more our breath spread over each other. Good way to keep warm. Our mouths were our own radiators now.

They used to march prisoners over the bridge, I said. *Corralled them together like cattle.*

Since when did you become such a history buff?

They went through the whole winter out here like that. Freezing. Starving.

Sounds familiar.

Slid in next to her. Nestled my knees into the backs of her legs, just where they bent. Had my face pressed against her shoulder, breathing into the bone.

They'd bring a surgeon out to check up on the men in the morning, figuring out which limbs he had to saw off from the frostbite.

Everybody in this city's a goddamn Civil War aficionado, she said, inching off without me. Figured that was the end of the conversation—up until Benny turned back around, asking, *So you gonna hold me, soldier? It's cold out here.*

Yes, captain.

Fell asleep first. I was always falling asleep before Benny—drifting off to the sound of her cough, these short retorts right at my ear, like some soldier in the trenches, the sound of musket fire just over my head.

I had brought my daughter to Belle Isle once.

Couldn't even tell you when anymore. Years ago.

A different life.

I had packed a picnic and everything. Had to get there early, just so we could lay claim to one of the broad rocks resting along the river. We're talking prime real estate here. You ended up battling the sunbathers for the best spread.

The Battle of Belle Isle.

Don't go out too far, hon, I had said. *You've got to be careful about the currents.*

Benny always had to hold me when I woke up. Wrap her arms around me so I didn't buckle, bringing me back to the present tense.

You're okay, you're okay, she'd say. *Just another bad dream, that's all.*

Everywhere you step on this island, there's another history lesson just under your feet. Signs saying what happened at that very spot, almost two hundred years ago. Nothing but plaques in the ground. Never would've realized this place could hold that much pneumonia. That much dysentery.

Richmond has too much history for its own good.

Whole city's a graveyard.

That's Richmond for you. It's only when you have no home to call your own that you can see this city for what it really is. You're standing on the graves of men no matter where you step.

The prison camp had been built directly below the highest mount on the island, overlooking the river. I remember bringing Benny up there, showing her the view for the first time. We could see the Capital building up north. To the west was Hollywood Cemetery, on the other side of the James. Petersburg wasn't but so far off, if you squinted hard enough.

Can't see why those soldiers wouldn't just swim for it, Benny said, shaking her head. *Lord knows I would.*

They'd try, I said. *End up getting shot right there in the water. Their bodies would drift downriver. Never set foot on dry land again.*

How do you know about all this stuff?

I just pay attention, is all. Pay attention. A good parent pays attention.

Let's go down there, she said, pointing toward the north side of the island.

Where?

Those big rocks—down there. Where the sunbathers all go.

I'm not setting foot down there, Benny.

Why not?

It's off-limits to us.

To me.

There's a dam still standing upstream, left over from the hydroelectric plant. Steers most of the water northward, around the bend and into the rapids. There are signs posted all around the island, warning families about the rapids. *Always have a parent supervising swimming children,* they say. *Don't let your kids go out too far unattended.* A bit of the river funnels south through this concrete canal, into what's left of the turbines. Used to generate enough electricity to light up half of Richmond back in the day.

Benny's body had slipped around the south, into the canal.

If she hadn't been dead when she entered the water, she was once she washed into the turbines. Her green paper gown was wrinkled, clinging to her skin like tissue paper. One sock on her left foot, nothing on the right. Reminded me of those sheep you see getting their coats shorn clean. Once the wool's been buzzed off their bodies, what's left behind seems so much smaller than what there was before. Pink skin. Thin frame. Legs don't even look real anymore.

I'm looking at Benny, lying on her side in the turbine—and I can't help but remember her all bulked up in her jackets, a layer of long johns underneath. She'd just gotten another new coat, three sizes too big for her. Pulled it out from the lost-and-found at some church. Made her look like a little girl wearing her daddy's jacket, her hands swallowed up by the sleeves.

Now she's naked. I'm seeing all the bruises I've never seen before, the abrasions. All the liver spots and melanomas that have been hidden from me. Her wrinkles are full of mud, as if the river has tried washing the years away. I've never seen her face look so smooth before. I can almost imagine what she looked like when she was a girl. Like in that photograph. The mud in her hair has dyed the white right out, changed her hair back to its natural brown. Chestnut eyes to match her new brunette curls.

I see the look in her eyes, glassed over—those last few thoughts that passed through her mind as she wrestled with the river, fighting for dry land.

Afraid. She looks like she had been afraid. I'm imagining her numb hands thrashing through the water, reaching for anything that's going to save her. She's wearing some sort of ID bracelet, orange plastic snapped into place. Her arms are so thin, nothing but skin and bones. The bracelet slides all the way up to her elbow.

Have her listed as DOE, JANE. Bastards even took her name away.

She'd been complaining about a cough all week. Hacking up phlegm in her sleep. Sounded awfully deep. Whatever it was, it was rooted in her chest, beginning to block her breathing. The air couldn't reach her lungs without sounding wet.

Jesus, Benny. You sound terrible. Think you better have that looked at.

You my doctor now? Where am I gonna go?

How about a hospital? I asked, pressing the back of my hand against her forehead.

Hospital? Nah. I'll sleep it off.

It was easy to feel the fever burning through. Felt so warm, I couldn't help but keep my hand there a little longer than I needed to. Hold onto that heat for a while. Couldn't help but think about all those soldiers, sitting in the cold. Sickest prisoners were always taken to the hospital just on the other side of the island. They were made to stand and wait until their names were taken. Could've been hours before they got called up. If they survived that long, they were led to a ward already cluttered with dozens of others. Sheets were never cleaned. Beds full of vermin. These doctors would rush through the ward like it was a race, seeing who could finish first. I never blamed Benny for distrusting doctors. But there she was, sounding like she was drowning from the inside out. Running her finger along the anchor tattooed on my arm as she sank deeper and deeper into her own lungs.

I'll go to the hospital if you let me ask you something . . .

Okay, I said. *Fire away.*

Why'd we really come here?

I didn't say anything.

What's so important about this place?

I made something up. Something about some Civil War relics buried somewhere around here. If we found them, we'd never have to worry over nothing ever again.

Hope you find it, she said, not buying it one bit, something pink making its way to her lips. *Whatever's buried here.*

Fell asleep first. I was always falling asleep before Benny did. Closed my eyes and found a familiar flame, this burning yellow one-piece, slipping off into the water without me.

Don't go too far out, hon, I'd said. *Only up to your ankles.*

We'd spread a blanket out across our rock. Lunch was behind us. All we had to do for the remainder of the day was rest next to the river. Take in the sun amongst all the other families. And swim.

But I want to go out there, Daddy . . .

Too dangerous, sweetie. You've got to be careful about the currents.

The what?

The currents!

Can't say how long I'd been sleeping. I didn't come to until I heard the family from the neighboring rock start shouting. I sat up, squinting against the sun. Couldn't focus at first, watching this flash of yellow disappear into the river.

Her body had turned blue by the time I reached her.

I dropped to my knees.

Pressed my lips against hers and breathed.

I tried pushing the air into her lungs. Her chest would expand. Her rib cage was a pair of ambulance doors fanning open. But the air only seeped out, her chest sinking back down again.

The air wouldn't stay inside my daughter.

Benny didn't wake me up the following morning. Didn't ease me up from my dream like she usually does. I had to snap back myself. Woke up and found her just next to me, barely breathing. Her eyes were wide open, staring up at nothing.

Benny . . . ? Benny, what's wrong?

I carried her across the underpass, back to the mainland. Hefted her the whole way to the hospital, just praying we'd make it. Lost the feeling in my arms, but I held onto her the whole time.

We're almost there, Benny, I said. *Almost there. Just hold on . . .*

The sliding glass doors parted, welcoming Benny inside. I rushed her right up to the front desk, out of breath. The nurse took one look at us and froze. Stared at me like I was holding up the place.

You've got to help her, I begged. *She's sick with something.*

What's her name? Do you know her name?

Benny, all right? Now just do something!

Spent fifteen minutes in the waiting room. Didn't take long to feel like I didn't belong. Looking over all the wounded, the sick. Everyone waiting for a doctor to call out their name. This little girl sitting next to me was scuffing her heels along the carpet. Her mom took one look at me and moved her daughter a couple rows over. Most folks were giving me a wide berth by then, sitting as far away as humanly possible. Caught sight of a couple security guards coming my way. The nurse from the front desk was following right behind them. Panic set into my system. Telling me I better act quick. But Benny wouldn't know where to go. She'd think I left her there.

The guards picked up their pace as soon as I stood up from my chair. I cut them off at the sliding glass doors. They followed me as far as the parking lot before giving up—while all the while, all I kept saying to myself was, *Belle Isle, Benny. Just meet me back at Belle Isle.*

Three days I wandered around. Took every nature path I could find, weaving in and out of the woods. I read every marker I stumbled upon until there wasn't a corner on this island where I didn't know exactly what had happened there. *Class was in session.* Time for my history lesson. Get up on my Richmond. Wait for Benny to come home.

The dead were buried on the western slope. That's what the sign said. Over a hundred prisoners of war dumped into the dirt. Nothing but burlap wrapped around their bones—the lice wriggling free, trying to hop out before the earth got shoveled over. The bodies remained on Belle Isle until 1864. Not long at all. Just a few years in the ground before they were dug back up and reinterred on the mainland. Their bones were taken away, while their ghosts got left behind.

Corporal Edwin Bissel from Iowa. Company D, fifth infantry.

Captain Spencer Deaton. Company B, Tennessee infantry.

Lieutenant J. T. Ketchum. Company M, Richmond artillery.

And now Benny.

Couldn't tell you where she was from. Couldn't say if she had any family around here or not. Never mentioned any kids of her own to me. But Benny was my friend. She's the only one buried on Belle Isle anymore. Her grave has gone unmarked. Her body rests inside the vacant spot of some dug-up soldier.

Only person who knows she's out there is me.

I stuffed her photographs into my pockets, layering up. Every jacket was padded with pictures, a Kevlar vest of Benny's memories to protect me.

I hadn't left Belle Isle for over a week. The footbridge felt like it was about to snap, rocking under the weight of the traffic passing overhead. I was a bit wobbly at first, setting foot back onto the mainland, as if I'd been at sea all this time.

First place I go was Monroe. Make an appearance for the police. Send a message that I'm looking for them. When you're after the brass, it's better to let them come to you. So I just rested myself on a bench along the northern portion of the park, right under a magnolia tree.

Couldn't have closed my eyes for more than an hour before I got my wake-up call. Nothing but a wooden baton in the ribs, two boys in blue encouraging me to move merrily along my way.

Time to get up, one of them said. *Sleep somewhere else.*

I'm looking for my friend.

Who's your friend?

Benny.

He loiter around here, too?

If I was going to find out what happened to Benny I knew I was going to have to go through it myself. Couldn't just waltz into the hospital and ask for a lollipop. The only way I was slipping past those sliding glass doors was with an emergency. And for that I needed a little help from my friends. So me and the boys in blue did a little Civil War reenactment of our own right there in the heart of Monroe Park. Sure were looking like soldiers to me, more and more, anyhow. Their cadet-blue uniforms. Their Jefferson boots. One stripe on their shoulder for every five years of faithful service. I went ahead and shoved my elbow into the stomach of the closest artilleryman. He buckled over, leaving me and the other soldier to share a few fists back and forth. Got a baton straight across the face. Busted my nose right open. Wasn't long before the other soldier got his breath back, swinging right along with the rest of us. Some swift hits to the stomach came my way. Then the chest. Before I knew it, I was on my knees, this heat swelling up in my gut.

We catch you in the park again—next time, we're arresting you.

Where's Benny?

Fed a few loose teeth to the pigeons. Spit them to the ground like bloody bread crumbs. Watched the birds scurry up, pecking away, even hungrier than me.

What'd you do to her? What did you do?!

Not gonna tell you again . . .

I blacked out after that. It gets a little patchy from here on. Memories begin to blend together. I'm mixing up my histories. It was pretty difficult to tell whose history was whose anymore.

I woke up in a waiting room. Could've been there for hours, staring up at the ceiling. Hum of fluorescents might as well have been flies buzzing about my body. Felt this fire inside my stomach. An oil lamp had busted open in my belly. Kerosene leaked from my spleen. Nurses hovering over my head. None of them liked the smell of me.

One of them said—*Got another homeless here.*

Speaking like I don't understand English.

Humana? UniCare?

Acting like they couldn't hear me—*Where's Benny?*

Blue Cross?

What'd you do with Benny?

Kept hearing the same word, over and over—*Insurance? Insurance?*

All I had was an eagle and an anchor.

Another asked—*Name?*

I answered back—*Lieutenant J. T. Ketchum. Company M, Richmond artillery.*

She called out—*This one's a vet, I guess.*

Damn right I'm a vet. I've got the tattoos to prove it. I served my country. I fought at the Battle of Belle Isle. I have defended this city all my life, I have given Richmond everything. My daughter. My best friend. I've got nothing now.

What's left of me to give?

My colon, apparently. Had something hooked up to my side—I

could feel it. A plastic bag. Reminded me one of Benny's bags with all her junk. One of Benny's bags was attached to my abdomen, itching like a son of a bitch. Every time I tried scratching, some nurse slapped my hand away.

Just trying to help—I said.

Help yourself is more like it—she said back, easing a needle into my arm. Suddenly the room went all soft. My tattoos felt fuzzy. The eagle on my forearm sank deeper into my skin, its talons dragging the earth down with it.

There's always something to lose. Just when you think you've got nothing left to give, there's always something more for this city to take away. Even your history. I'm back at the prison camp. Gangrene's lingering in the air. Rotten cheese. Got to keep the flies off—otherwise, they'll lay their eggs in my wounds. Neglected men everywhere, suffering from exposure. Fingers and feet lost to frostbite. Typhoid fever. Dysentery. My miserable comrades are dying all around me as the morning shift takes over, new nurses asking the same questions—*Anthem?*

What'd you do to Benny?

CareFirst?

What'd you do to my friend?

Clothes are gone. My shoes are gone. Got me in this green paper gown now.

Green paper gown. *Green paper gown!*

I'm in a wheelchair, rolled out into the parking lot. It's morning. Sun's just rising. An ambulance pulls up in front of me. I'm told to hold my colostomy bag as it drops into my lap. Feels soft inside. The guy behind the wheel asks for an address.

Where you want to go? You got to give me an address, pal . . .

Only address that's coming to mind is Freedom House. On Hull.

There's no shelter on Hull anymore, he says as we drive off. *Shut that one down a long time ago.*

The ambulance stops. Back doors fan open. I'm met with the winter sun. I can see my breath fog up before me. I see the James.

I see the river.

Richmond couldn't have cared less about Benny. They dumped her along the river—up and dumped her as far away from themselves as they could, hoping the currents would carry her the rest of the way. What happened to her must happen in that hospital all the time. Because here it is, happening to me.

The driver won't let me keep the wheelchair. All I get is my colostomy bag. He tosses a ziplock next to me, full of photographs. None of these faces look familiar. Can't tell if they're my family or not. I slip the edge of the pouch between my teeth, carrying it in my mouth as I crawl across the rocks.

My green paper gown softens in the water. Adheres itself to my body like a second layer of skin. The river's cold—but before long, all feeling is gone. I know I'm moving, I know I'm on my back. I can see my arms fanning through the water. My colostomy bag must be keeping me afloat, bobbing along the surface. Everything I own is inside.

A few photographs loosen themselves from the ziplock between my teeth, floating along the water without me. Suddenly I'm surrounded by spinning pictures, swirling over the surface, moving downstream.

One picture floats up in front of me. Black and white. Cute little brunette smiling for the camera. Reminds me of someone I used to know. Lost her along this river, long ago. Never been able to get her back. And here's history repeating itself all over again, like getting caught in a whirlpool. Sucking me under.

Looking at that photograph, bobbing through the water—I'm watching my daughter swim downriver with me, the two of us drifting along together.

That's Richmond for you.

This city's built upon bones. What isn't buried simply washes downriver.

I just got to hit the right current. Ease myself to the southern side of the James. Keep to the right and I'll make it.

Got to make my way back to Belle Isle.

Got to head home.

GHOST
STORIES

b-side

We are the hi-fi pioneers. The sonic ethnographers. The audio archeologists, unearthing the unheard.

We will dig through any estate sale, any church fundraiser, any dust-covered, sun-bleached flea market milk crate in order to excavate those rarest of recordings.

The juke joint jams. The field recordings. The medicine shows and minstrel acts. We're talking *deep blues* here. Deeper than anyone's ever dug up before. To be able to say you exhumed a long-lost recording, heard only by a handful of folks—that's better than bragging rights. That's history in your hands.

You're holding a sonic artifact, son. Nobody's ears in the last fifty years have heard these 78s. *Eighty years.* These singers may as well be crooning just to you.

It's not my heritage—*fine.*

But ask any rare-record collector where he dug up his 78s and nine times out of ten, he'll tell you the same thing: He found them mildewing in somebody's basement. Stashed in the attic. Hidden in the closet. Practically in the trash already.

All I'm doing? All I'm doing is disinterring what's dead already.

I'm bringing the blues back from the grave, one lost record at a time.

Single Copy Only.

That meant Bo-Lita Dean. Or Riverview Blue. Possibly even— *please Jesus,* let it be Bessie Brown. The holy grail of all 78s could've been buried at the back of some cobwebbed milk crate at the Copiah County Flea Market, lost for all these years between a warped Tijuana Brass LP and Tom Jones: *Live in Las Vegas.*

There was no label on the disc. No artist's name anywhere. The unmarked sleeve was a faded butcher-paper brown, rubber-stamped with the red initials . . .

S.C.O.

Say it with me one more time: *Single Copy Only.* As in, the master recording. No duplicates. The one and only original, right here in my hands.

Rule number one for flea marketing: *Never let on like you know what you're holding.* If a dealer sniffs you out, better expect a solid seventy percent mark-up before you can even begin to haggle. But act casual enough and you'll end up paying fifty cents for a long-forgotten Fats Plateau. Two bucks for a near-mint condition Blind Birdie Rose.

Lord only knows who the mystery musician was on this record. My best guess? It was a Wardlow Wiley one-off.

Wiley wasn't a musician. He was the proprietor of his own prewar race-records label—Wiley's Negro Spirituals and Field

Recordings. He was just some white guy who ran his family hardware store straight into the ground after a misguided try at moonlighting in the music business. After closing up shop for the day, he'd pile his recording equipment into the back of his flatbed and make his way through Mississippi in the middle of the night, hopping from one back-alley brothel to the next in order to record whatever blues singer was strumming for customers that night.

A recently rediscovered 78 from his label can fetch up to four to five thousand nowadays . . . *If* you're lucky enough to find one.

You always know when you're listening to one of Wiley's 78s, thanks to a particular auditory anomaly found only on his recordings. An echo effect. Sets his pressings aside from the rest.

What is it? Take a guess.

The toilet. Bathrooms had the best acoustics, he found. The closest thing to a recording studio on the road was the crapper. Wiley would set up his equipment in one wooden stall, sitting his singer on the neighboring toilet—and away they'd go. On some tracks you can actually hear the fists of plastered patrons banging against the bathroom door. At the tail end of Geechie Gulliver's "Train Done Gone for the Day," the fortuitously timed flush of a toilet sounds like a slow brushstroke against a snare, washing the song away.

If this was one of Wiley's discs, there's no telling whose voice was on here.

That one's not for sale, sugar . . .

The lot owner sat sweating away in a lawn chair at the front of her stall, fanning herself like some overweight Madame Butterfly

in a muumuu. She was hooked up to an oxygen tank, those clear
rubber tubes branching out from her nostrils like a pair of catfish
whiskers. One hand rested on the nozzle of her oxygen, palming
it as if it were a plantation owner's cane—a Pall Mall nestled between her knuckles.

This one doesn't seem to have a dust jacket, I said. *Any idea who's
on it?*

That . . . ? That's Pigmeat Mays.

Never heard of him.

Never would, she huffed. *You're holding his only record. Been
looking high and low for it. Thought I'd lost it. Shouldn't even be out.*

Lucky I found it then, I said. *How much you want for it?*

Rule number two: *Always let the dealer set the price.* Never start
bargaining by laying down a number before they do. This lady
didn't strike me as a rare Delta blues connoisseur, but I'm betting
she'd dealt with her fair share of scavengers before. I'd already
spotted a handful of DJs swooping down on the flea market that
morning. Nothing but vultures pecking at all the choice cuts—the
rare groove records, the old soul and long forgotten proto-rhythm
and blues, covered in dust, the very vinyl wilting from countless
hours of sitting under the pummeling Mississippi sun.

But a 78 like this lands in your hands only once in a lifetime.

*Records tend to disappear till they're ready to be rediscovered
again, all on their own.* She coughed. *But that one there's better left
buried, believe you me.*

I'll take it off your hands for, uh . . . ten.

She leaned back in her lawn chair to let her lungs flex in her
chest, easing her wheezing for a spell. *You're another one of those*

crate diggers, aren't you? Always sounded like "gravedigger" to me. Crate robber's more like it . . .

How about fifteen?

I said it's not for sale, son. Not for you.

Twenty.

Wanna hear a broken record? Ask me one more time.

I'm only going up to thirty now. Final offer. Probably not worth more than a couple bucks anyhow.

Try priceless. She took a puff from her Pall Mall, straining to inhale, the smoke spiriting out from her mouth as she spoke. *There's a ghost on that record, boy. Listen to it and you'll hear what the dead sound like when they sing . . .*

What happened to Wardlow Wiley?

Depends who you ask. Some say he hung himself after his little music venture bankrupted his hardware business. Another version had him vanishing into thin air, leaving his family behind to pay his debts. Another had his body popping up in a ditch one morning in Woodmere, throat slit ear to ear and bled out like a pig.

Whatever you believe, if this 78 was actually one of his recordings, chances are, only a handful of people had ever listened to it.

Time to authenticate.

Give me a history lesson on Pigmeat Mays.

Pigmeat? Jimmy intoned into the phone. *Not much to tell, really . . . Butcher by trade, blues singer by night. Started off picking cotton*

*like everybody else. But when the weevils knocked out all the crops,
he moved on to meat. Hence the name.*

If there was anything I didn't know about a record, rare as that
sounds, I'd put in a call to Jimmy. That's how good he was.

*There's a rumor Pigmeat did his own version of "Boll Weevil
Blues," he said.*

You mean Old Crow Cochran's "Boll Weevil Blues?"

*Yeah—but Pigmeat put his own spin on it, apparently. Tinkered
with the lyrics a bit till it fit his rhythm. Slowed it down.*

Everybody knows how Cochran's rendition went. Simple fingerpicking. It opens up with a hefty E before retreating into an A
minor. The chorus went:

Gas-o-line is the only thing, gas-o-line is the only thing,
Gasoline is the only thing that keeps these here crops clean,
And burns these weevils a-way . . .

I plucked that 78 out of a milk crate at a Texarkana yard sale.
Cost me thirty cents. Now it runs upward to two, maybe three
thousand bucks.

Jimmy had literally wept, just bawled like a baby, after I played
it for him over the phone. You'd cry too if you heard Old Crow
Cochran sing. The metal masters of his recordings are probably
insulating somebody's attic right about now. Only three copies of
his 78 survived. Mine was a mere five feet away from where I was
sitting just then, stacked in my living room right alongside Nehe-
miah James, Booker J. Graves, Johnny Rawls. Over five hundred
meticulously categorized records.

A sonic mausoleum.

Why so curious about Pigmeat Mays? Jimmy asked. *You found something?*

Just interested.

All that's left of him is a Wardlow Wiley recording, allegedly . . . But we may as well be talking about a unicorn here, man. It just doesn't exist.

How'd Wiley get his hands on him?

Story goes Wiley stumbled upon Mays right outside of Jackson. Word got around about his singing style. More Tommy Tenderfoot than Robert Watkins, you know? Like a bullfrog praising God on every croak. Wiley just waltzed right into the meat-processing plant where Mays slaughtered cattle and asked if he wanted to lay down a couple sides with him. They did the recording right there in the meat locker.

You're lying.

Hand to God. Used the hanging racks of halved beef as impromptu soundproofing and everything. Mays never even pulled off his apron. Wore that leather bib while Wiley recorded his song "Killing Floor Shuffle," strumming his slide guitar until . . .

Jimmy's voice trailed off.

What?

The B-side was gonna be Pigmeat's rendition of "Boll Weevil Blues," but before Wiley could record it . . . Well, supposedly, Mays just keeled over. Heart attack. Died right there. Wiley panicked, packed up his equipment and ran off. He just left Mays's body behind. They didn't find him until the next morning, all frozen in the fridge.

You're telling me Pigmeat May's was Wiley's last recording?

Not that anyone's ever heard it.

Know anybody who has?

Can't say I know anybody. Jimmy sighed into the receiver. *You'd have an easier time finding the Dead Sea Scrolls in the Mississippi River than somebody who's listened to a Pigmeat pressing before. But you better believe I'd travel five hundred miles just to give it a whirl if it ever popped up . . .*

Three hundred and eighty five miles is my personal record.

A 45 of Skip Tilly's "Boiler Room Ya-Ya" had resurfaced in Piedmont a few years back, so I hopped on a Greyhound down to Virginia. Knocked on the owner's door and asked if I could give it a spin. He kindly obliged, putting the record on.

I listened once and left.

But for that whole bus ride back, all I could hear was the hiss and crackle of the needle burrowing through the groove. That wildfire of vinyl. And the voice that lifted off the record, like smoke—once you heard Tilly sing, his breath never left you.

You've got it, don't you? Jimmy whispered into the receiver, mock conspiratorially, as if someone else was listening in on the line. *How'd you find it?*

Barking up the wrong tree here, man . . .

Come on. Just tell me you've got it.

Say I did. How much would you lay down for it?

We're talking hypothetically here?

For argument's sake.

Five hundred.

For an S.C.O.? I'm hanging up . . .

Fine, fine—two thousand. I'd go up to two thousand.

Five.

Back at the flea market, I had dropped three bucks on some bullshit Marlene Flemming/Judah Bay Blues split 7-inch before heading onto the next stall, simply to save face with Madame Butterfly.

Actually, just the sleeve.

Can't even bring myself to touch the damned thing, she had said. *You put it back in the bin right where you found it and forget it even exists, you hear?*

So somebody else can grab it?

That record's not for you. It's not for anyone.

I put the Pigmeat Mays back in the bin, as instructed, but not before a little switcheroo when the lady was lighting up a fresh Pall Mall. She never stood up from her lawn chair, letting customers come to her. The closer I got with that Pigmeat in my hands, the more the wet rasp from her lungs sounded like the sizzle and spit of a needle raking over a record. I made sure to smile after we made our exchange.

Pleasure doing business, ma'am . . .

Pigmeat was all mine.

Let me listen, Jimmy pleaded. *Just play it for me over the phone. Just once.*

Hand to God, Jimmy, I don't have it.

'Cause the kicker is, they say Wiley recorded Pigmeat's last breath on the B-side. If that's the sort of thing you believe. Listen to it and you can hear him croak.

I've been listening to ghosts all my life. What's one more musician haunting me?

Time to have ourselves a little listening party . . .

I've perfected a particular listening ritual for myself. You've got to savor these sounds. Like a fine wine, you know? *Don't guzzle it.* You can only listen to an excavated 78 for the first time once, so lock all the doors. Turn the phone off. Set up the hi-fi in the living room, wallpapered with LPs, and settle in for the night.

I'd fired up the turntable. Wiped down the disc with alcohol and ammonia, cleaning out the steel fillings from all the previous record needles. These original gramophone records were pressed from shellac. Long before vinyl came around, the scarlet resin secreted from the female lac beetle was the main compound in capturing that Delta sound, reinforced with a little cotton flock. That makes these discs pretty brittle a half century later. Use the wrong kind of stylus and you could scrape away the last known recording of Pigmeat Mays forever. *Good as ghosted.*

Side A had been a raw number. Some primitive little ditty titled "Killing Floor Shuffle." No production value to the recording whatsoever. Somebody coughs in the background. Probably Wardlow Wiley. Leaning in and listening close, I imagined Mays's breath fogging over in the meat locker as he sang into Wiley's mic.

I closed my eyes and disappeared into the recording. The lyrics were a bit difficult to decipher, but the chorus went something like . . .

Too much blood on this here killing floor,
Watch them butchers slip back and forth,

Leg's a-sliding, causing so much trouble,
Dancing that killing floor shuffle.

I'm there. In the freezer. I can nearly hear the drop in temperature within the recording itself, bitter to my ear. It's crisp in here. My lungs seem to have crystallized themselves. It burns to even breathe. The only warmth comes from Mays's voice as he sings just over my shoulder. I swear I can feel his breath spread down my neck.

I don't know how much time passed between the song ending and me opening my eyes, but the room spun a bit before settling back down again.

Time for the B-side. An accidental field recording. None other than Mays's own ghost, captured in shellac.

Flipping the record over, I slipped the disc back onto the turntable. I pinched the tonearm, one breath away from sinking the needle.

Let's give the ghost of Pigment Mays a spin. Hear what he has to say.

Only my wrist locked.

The needle hovered above the record. I watched the 78 whirl on the turntable. Soundless. Just yearning for the needle to give it voice. I got lost in the grooves of the record, swirling hypnotically round and round and round and . . .

I lowered the needle into the groove.

I closed my eyes and leaned back, letting the sizzle and pop fill up the room.

And then . . .

Static. Ten seconds into the B-side and there wasn't much else to hear. Just the sibilant hiss of the stylus digging a trench through the shellac.

So much for ghosts.

I sat back up, just about to check the record, when a muddy rasp at the back of Pigmeat May's throat suddenly lifted up from the speakers.

It was barely audible above the crackle of static—but there it was.

A death rattle.

Then it grew louder. A guttural lunge at my ears. It sounded as if someone was reaching for the speakers, *through the speakers*, crawling up from the recording and into the room with me.

It sounded like he was getting closer.

I yanked the tonearm off. The needle raked over the record, scraping at the shellac—and just for a moment, it sounded like muscle tearing away from the bone.

Please, please tell me I didn't just destroy a goddamn S.C.O....

My head felt fuzzy. The back of my throat was suddenly dry. Cottonmouth.

I was about to head to the kitchen for a drink when I felt this itch in my ear. I swatted at it, figuring it's just a fly. Only the tickle went deep. This persistent scurry was in the inner lobe. I pawed at the side of my head like a dog scratching for fleas.

DDTs did away with the weevil back in the '50s—so it took me a moment to recognize what had just crawled out of my ear.

A little history lesson on boll weevils:

Boll weevils were the muse for blues musicians all through Mississippi. That pest would lay its eggs inside an entire crop's worth of cotton buds, the larvae eating their way out. Millions of dollars worth of cotton fields were chewed through.

The only things more abundant than an infestation of weevils back in the '20s were the number of songs written about them. Everybody remembers Buster Guthrie's "Ballad of the Boll Weevil"—but don't forget Texas Elliott's "The Boll Weevil Song."

Or Chester Henry's "The Evil in the Weevil."

Or The Mississippi All-Star Revue's "Mississippi Boll Weevil."

Or Sally Mae Jane's "The 1923 Boll Weevil Upheaval."

There's no telling what Pigmeat's cover of "Boll Weevil Blues" would've sounded like if he'd actually had the chance to record the song before keeling over.

But I think I might have a good idea.

The weevil landed in my lap. It was on its mustard-brown back, all six legs swimming through the air like a baby about to have its diaper changed. A slender antenna was situated at the anterior of its head, branching off into separate elbows.

Where in the hell did that come from?

Lord only knows how long I stared at it. The hum of the turntable rotating on its own lulled me off, away from the room.

I only snapped back when a second weevil scuttled out from my ear.

Listen.

Listen closely.

Listen closely and you can hear them.

Sitting around the fire.

In the kitchen.

On the front porch.

Fingerpicking their six-strings. Heels tapping on the front steps, the wood warping beneath their boots. Field hands serenading one another through the night after a long day in the crops, cicadas singing right along.

The loose laments.

The raw songs.

Listen closely and you can hear the acoustics of the rooms. The negative space around the sound. What's *not* being sung captured on the recording as well.

The ambient drone of locusts during a Mississippi dusk, 1939.

The clatter of dishes in the kitchen sink, 1924.

The clearing of a throat before the voice belts away, 1897.

It's all there, the sonic geography of the moment when these songs were recorded. A prehistoric insect trapped in amber, preserved within the very vinyl.

I rushed into the bathroom and quickly found my reflection in the cabinet mirror. What was left of it. My face was eclipsed by a swarm boiling out from my ear. I could see the weevils crawling across my cheeks. My forehead. My mouth. I made the mistake of making a sound, cracking my lips open just enough to moan, only to feel their segmented legs scrape against my tongue. As soon as I swatted a handful away, another dozen would scurry over my skin and take their place. Burying me.

I remember reading that a mother weevil can lay up to two hundred eggs in a single crop. Sounds about right. It's a verifiable anthill in my ear right now. I've got the blues bubbling up from the canal, eating its way out through the lobe.

How'd that song go again?

Gas-o-line is the only thing, gas-o-line is the only thing,
Gasoline is the only thing that keeps these here crops clean,
And burns these weevils a-way . . .

He may as well have been crooning just for me.

I can feel them.

All the songs.

The revenant recordings, brought back from the dead.

At first, I plugged up my ears with cotton balls—but they chewed through. I tried plucking them out with a pair of tweezers. Watched them squirm. They'd wriggle out from my grip just as ten more would crawl out from my ear canal.

Twenty. Thirty.

Most of the songs have all hatched by now. There are too many to count.

Now I have no choice but to let them all sing.

Every time I listen to the record, I swear I hear something different. It's a new song every time.

Pigmeat sounded much closer to the microphone on the second spin.

On the third, the depth of his breath had changed.

He must be growing stronger.

I'll let the 78 play to the end, the turntable churning out an even tide of static, waves lapping at the shore. When I realize it's been spinning for hours, I'll bring the tonearm back to the beginning of the record and lower the stylus all over again.

And again. And again and again and . . .

The walls are writhing in brown bodies. The room hums now. Hundreds of vibrating wings. Every step I take has a slight crunch underneath it. I've watched the weevils weave in and out of my record stacks, chewing through the vinyl.

My collection is gone.

The only record left is Pigmeat's S.C.O., swirling on the turntable. None of them will touch it.

He's coming. Won't be much longer. He'll be here before you know it.

Soon. *Very soon.*

On the twentieth listen, I could've sworn he was standing right behind me, breathing down my neck.

On the fiftieth, he whispered into my ear.

He's here now. I can see him.

He's reaching for me. He's holding out his hand. His fingers seem to be nothing more than insects, breaking apart and squirming back together again.

What does he want?

Simple. He wants my undivided attention. He wants to make sure I'm all ears.

What's he saying?

This is not your music. These songs are not for you.

All I can hear anymore is the hiss of the needle racing through the groove, hundreds of wings brushstroking against my eardrum. A hive in the mind.

I just can't get this song out of my head.

split ends

Died right there on the dance floor. Saw it with my own two eyes. That frizzy-haired *puta* had been grabbing her ankles all night, rubbing up against whichever motherfucker's close enough. The superglue holding her hair extensions to the rest of her head started to leach through her scalp, seeping into her bloodstream and—

BAM. Anaphylactic shock.

Motherfuckers circled around while she just slipped into convulsions, like she's an epileptic on *Soul Train.* Her ass spazzing on down the dance floor. Kept clawing at her throat, foaming up Red Bull and Hennessy.

D to the *O* to the motherfucking *A.*

Paramedics called it on the spot. Said that bitch had an allergic reaction to her own nappy-ass weave.

¡Lo siento, nena!—but that's what you get for wearing synthetic. *Plastico.* Barbie doll hair.

¡Ay de mi! Her stylist should be dragged out into the street by her own extensions and shot in front of every last one of her dumbass customers.

Wasn't my fault she picked acrylic. Wasn't one of my clientele, was she? You don't see me supergluing highly toxic latex to your head, now, do you?

Natural hair or *nada*.

I will never sew one synthetic hair onto your head, you hear me? I will never come near your scalp with one bit of acrylic. You want your weave to feel like it's yours, *solo tuyo*, as if each and every last one of those hairs grew out from your skull.

I can make that happen. 'Cause you're a queen in my court. This here chair's your throne, girl. You sit with me—the second you stand, you are wearing a crown.

So claim what's rightfully yours, Your Majesty . . .

Your throne awaits.

The crown is yours.

Normally, now, I wouldn't be divulging this much information. *Loose lips sink a bitch.* Nobody wants to know where their hair comes from. It's yours now. That's all that matters. Think of the head that wore it before you as a surrogate scalp. You are now the proud parent of these luxurious, silky smooth, full-bodied locks . . .

But we got ourselves a little *stylist-patient confidentiality* going on here.

Between you and me?

I'm not only the Hair Club president, I'm also a client . . .

Check this shit out. Pull on it.

Go ahead. Give a tug.

Thought it was mine, right? Everybody does. Nobody can tell the difference. *Nobody.* That's 'cause it's real. We're talking human hair. None of that synthetic shit.

If I can't rock my own product, what kinda stylist am I?

But the demand for that virgin-cuticle hair? That top-shelf shit? So fucking high, mother-come-fuck-me—I can't afford to pay those prices. These hair-collecting *hijos de putas* are charging two hundred dollars for one ponytail. *Doscientos* for twenty inches of hair? Some village girl in India or wherever shaves her fucking head for five cents and now I've got to pay half of a week's wage for it? Fuck that.

I'll go my own way, *muchas gracias.*

I'll find my own hair.

Took me two years to stand right here. *La puta* who runs this dump rents out the last three seats in her salon. She don't give a greasy shit how you pay, just as long as you do. *In cash. On time.* You're late with her money, *BAM*, your ass is back braiding hair on the street. *Bruja* even dips into our tip jar when we're not looking.

You want to succeed in this business, you need a chair.

Straight up.

You want your own chair, you need customers. A clientele you call your own. And the only way you get clients for life is to have what none of these other motherfucking *lagarta stylistas* got.

And what've I got, but top-quality product at rock-bottom prices?

We're talking natural hair.

Human hair.

And for the freshest, for that *natural* shit, you got to head directly on down to the *depósito de cadáveres.*

When I first met Reggie at the club, first words out of his mouth was that he worked at the coroner's office. I was all like—*Fuck that, you sick psycho son of a bitch. You call that a come-on?* I could smell the embalming fluid still on him, like it was cologne or whatever, sweating through his silk shirt. *Don't come grabbing at me with those clammy-ass hands. Not after you been feeling up dead bodies all damn day.*

But then I was like—*Hold up. Don't be so hasty, lady. This might be a business opportunity come knocking right here, asking me if I want to dance.*

Know how many unclaimed bodies there are in this city?

Fucking hundreds. Thousands. People dying all the time? All those Jane Does with their hair, just going to waste in the morgue with nobody looking for them? No family, no friends, no nobody. After ninety days—*BOOM*. Your time's up. You got yourself an appointment with the crematorium.

So I ask Reggie—*What happens to all that hair?*

He says—*Burns with the rest, baby. The roof, the roof, the roof is on fire!*

Took that *coño* two more Coronas to muster up the nuts to ask— *My place or yours?*

I went ahead and said—*How about you take me back to the morgue,* amante*?*

Rule *numero uno*: Always carry a condom and pack a pair of hair clippers in your purse, wherever you go. Plus an extra pair of panties. You never know where you're going to end up or when you're going to need them—am I right, ladies?

Wasn't like Jane Doe was going to miss her hair. She was all kinds of messed up. Puerto Rican girl. Couldn't have been any older than sixteen. Reggie's suddenly getting all squeamish on me. Wouldn't tell me what happened to her, but I know a knife wound when I see one. I counted six slits in her skin, each one looking like an open mouth, like when you're just about to say something, the words on the tip of your tongue, but as soon as you open your mouth to start speaking, they're not there anymore, like—*Uuuh, uuum, uuuuh* . . .

But her hair? *Ay dios mio.* That shit was *beautiful.* Black pearl. All down her back. We're talking fifteen, twenty inches, easy. Those drabby-ass fluorescents made the morgue look like an aquarium. Sucked the color right out of her skin. But I swear I saw her hair swirl. Like there were other colors mixed in with it. A whole rainbow.

Ever see pictures of oil spills in Alaska or New Orleans or wherever? You get those pelicans wrestling with the polluted water? I ran my fingers through that girl's hair and it wouldn't let me go. My hand came back wrapped in ropes of black, swear to God. Had to imagine myself on one of those cleaning crews, like I'm an environmentalist or whatever, skimming up that oil slick with my clippers—*Bzzzzz.*

Jane Doe's nothing but ash by now. There's a shoe box somewhere holding a ziplock bag filled with whatever bone particles didn't burn up with the rest of her.

But her hair . . . ? That shit lives on.

I got my own fusion technique. I attach each extension to a strand of your own hair, sectioning off a lock about a quarter of an inch thick, as thin a thread as possible, for that extra-natural look. I'll dip the cuticle's tip into this keratin adhesive. Just my own lil' secret sauce. Family recipe. All it takes to fuse the two together is a heat clamp, melting the keratin to your own hair—and voilà: You're a new woman now.

Look at you.

Just *look.*

Ever seen hair as black as that? Heads will be turning your way the second you step out of this salon, I swear. Nobody—*nadie*—is going to be able to tell where your hair stops and where this weave starts.

This hair's yours now, Your Majesty. All yours.

You two are inseparable.

Let's talk about upkeep, okay? You've got about three months of wearing this weave before you're going to need to come see me again. You can wash it, use hair products in it. I'd recommend a protein deep conditioner. Some of that cocoa keratin soothing shampoo will do the trick. If your weave starts to feel loose around the roots, just call me and I'll re-fuse the strands back to your natural hair. *Good as new.*

You might start hearing things. Whispers or whatever. Some of my customers have complained they've heard voices coming from over their shoulder. I got this one *puta* coming back at me after she's been wearing her extensions for less than a week. She's freaking the fuck out, swearing somebody's whispering in her ear all the time when ain't nobody there, yelling at me like it's my job to do something about it.

What the fuck do you want me to do? Call the loony bin for you?

This voice, she says, it seeps into her ears. The warmth of their breath spreads right down the lobe, like somebody's standing right behind her, just leaning in over her shoulder, their lips only inches away from her ear.

And this voice, it reaches in deep. Burrows into her brain. It won't let go.

Whispering things like—*Ayudame.*

Or—*Para, por favor. Para.*

You got to take care of your new hair now.

Protect it.

Cherish it.

Love it like it was your own. Give it the life it never had before, cut short by some son-of-a-bitch boyfriend with a kitchen knife. Gets her in the chest. The shoulder. The neck. All the while, she's begging him to stop—*Para, por favor.*

Calling out—*ayuda, ayuda*—but her voice chokes in her throat, her punctured lung filling up with blood, drowning from the inside out.

Everybody heard. Whole fucking apartment building heard her scream *but not one of those motherfuckers did a thing. Just locked their doors and listened . . .*

That little girl? Miss Jane Doe?

She's lonely. *Cold.*

She tells me things. Whispers them in my sleep.

In my dreams, I'll see those slits in her skin. Each one of them opens and closes, like lips, all those knife wounds saying the same thing . . .

Ayudame. Para, por favor. Para.

Did you know that your hair continues to grow even after you're dead? Death doesn't stop it from growing. Extending. Reaching out for you.

Jane Doe isn't so lonely anymore, now that I've found *customers for life.*

She's all yours now. Her hair, your hair, our hair now.

She's an extension of yourself.

diary debris

Pages from an Israeli astronaut's diary that survived the explosion of the space shuttle Columbia and a 37-mile fall to earth are going on display this weekend for the first time in Jerusalem.

—Associated Press, 2008

Ilan Ramon kept his diary in between his knees when reentering the earth's atmosphere. For the last sixteen days of his life, his diary had drifted right alongside him at zero gravity—always floating close enough for him to scribble down another journal entry whenever he wanted.

Day three: It's easy to keep kosher in outer space when all you have to eat is thermo-stabilized eggplant.

And—*Day six: Today's the first day I feel like I am truly living in space. I have become a man who lives and works in outer space.*

His handwriting at zero gravity was much better than mine back down here on the ground in Miss Plymouth's fifth-grade English class, even if most of his was in Hebrew. At first, I couldn't figure out just what it was that I was reading. Felt like I'd found some long-lost book of alien secrets written in an extraterrestrial cryptogram, fallen right out from the sky.

You just don't come across that many Jews down here in Palestine, Texas, is all.

Grady, honey, Mom had said to me. *Why don't you say grace for us tonight?*

Someone kicked me under the table. I kept quiet until my five older sisters and my one older brother all bowed their heads, making sure everybody had closed their eyes and brought their hands up to their chins before beginning our blessing.

Yom Ha-shishi, I mispronounced in my best Hebrew-before-realizing-I-was-even-speaking-Hebrew, repeating the prayer Ilan Ramon had written in his diary to recite onboard the space shuttle *Columbia* for the Sabbath while he was still in orbit. *Va-ye-chulu hasha-mayim vi-ha-aretz vi-kole tzi-va-am . . .*

Mom called upon Father Tom before I could even finish the kiddush, crying into our telephone that I was suddenly speaking in tongues at the dinner table. He rushed out to our house before my meal could grow cold, ready for an exorcism. Took one look at me picking at my green beans, half-expecting me to spit pea soup into his eye—*So what've we gotten ourselves into this time, Grady?*

Va-ye-varech Elohim es yom hashe-vi'i va-yi-kadesh oso . . .

That's not the devil, ma'am, Father Tom said, shaking his head.
Then what is it?

I believe your son's speaking . . . Hebrew.

Mom turned toward my siblings, all six of them peeking their heads through the kitchen door—*When in the world did my eleven-year-old boy start speaking Hebrew?*

An air bubble had swelled up from the insulation layer in the shuttle's left wing during liftoff. A scrap of fuel-tank foam broke off from inside the capsule and crumbled into flaming bits, cracking the wing's thermal protection layer on its way up into outer space. Once the Columbia began its return to earth, that fissure only cracked further back. All that scalding hot gas from the atmosphere slipped inside the insulation layer, *inside* the wing—this immense heat suddenly seeping into the shuttle, the entire spacecraft instantly disintegrating just above my head. An even streak of fire reached across the sky. Bits of burning debris broke off and flared out, like a dandelion someone had just blown on. All its seeds burst into the air. Fragments of its fuselage dispersed over two thousand square miles of Texas prairie land.

Commander Rick Husband. Pilot Willie McCool. Michael P. Anderson. Laurel Clark. David Brown. Kalpana Chawla. And Ilan Ramon. Nothing but dandelion snow now, all of them picked up by the wind, their remains scattering throughout the atmosphere.

I remember the horizon had gone all orange, same bright carroty color as the astronauts' space suits. I'd woken up before the sun had even come up, tiptoeing over my brothers and sisters to set up my telescope in the cattle field neighboring our backyard. Our house is situated directly underneath NASA's interstellar landing strip, that span of airspace extending from the Pacific Ocean all the way to Kennedy Space Center. Ground control ushers shuttles into Florida just above our backyard.

Only thing more vast than the expanse of prairie land stretching over the rest of Texas is outer space. Makes it simple for a kid to want to grow up and become an astronaut. What else is there? If you're not looking out across the endless stretch of grassy plains surrounding you, you're probably tilting your head up to the stars.

I had come running into Mom's room right after the explosion. She woke up with a start, finding me sobbing into the bedspread right by her hip.

Grady—what happened? What's wrong?

The sky's on fire, Mom, I cried. *They're all burning up there.*

I've been the youngest of seven kids my whole life. That's the exact same number of crew members onboard the *Columbia*. We're all crammed inside the tight confines of our one-story clapboard house, about as cramped as that cockpit. You better believe I'd take space over these prairies any day. I've got the moon-landing posters to prove it. My diet's mainly comprised of astronaut ice cream. I've even got my bedroom plastered in a glow-in-the-dark solar system. All these star stickers smolder over the ceiling as soon as my mother kisses me good night and flicks off the light. I'll stay awake in bed, just looking upward, until that greenish lightning-bug glow fades from the walls, all the phosphorescent constellations seeping back into the ceiling again. For those few minutes just after the lights go out, it's like I'm sleeping under the stars. No roof over my head anymore. Just the whole solar system. Nothing but space in every which direction.

Observing the Sabbath in outer space is much harder than you might think. *Jerusalem—we have a problem . . .* The gap between sunrises in orbit lasts only about ninety minutes, which meant Ilan Ramon only had an hour and a half for his Saturday.

You mowed the lawn yet, Grady? Mom called from the kitchen. *Or are you still watching cartoons?*

It's the Sabbath, Ma . . . I can't work on the day of rest.

Sabbath? she yelled. *What the hell is your little brother going on about now?*

They recovered the remains of a crew member in Nacogdoches. Some kid in Sabine County had come across a scorched leg in his backyard. A charred helmet. A mission patch with the *Columbia* insignia stitched across it. A hazmat team quickly picked up all the bits and pieces and sent them to Johnson Space Center in Houston for proper identification. The news that night reported that the Israel Defense Forces were sending some military rabbinate specialist to Texas to help try and identify the remains of Ilan Roman, separating his body parts from the rest of the crew. Since he was Israel's first astronaut, his remains needed to be treated according to Jewish tradition, with as much of him as possible returned back home for a proper burial.

Grady—go to your room, Mom had said. *I don't want you watching this.*

But Ma . . .

No buts about it. You're too young to listen to all this talk about bodies. You're only gonna end up giving yourself more nightmares.

I tried finding Israel on my gyromatic meridian-mounted world globe. Took me a while to pinpoint it with my finger, scanning over the raised-relief landforms and countries differentiated by color scheme—eventually coming upon this little sliver of land situated all the way on the other side of the world.

Talk about small. Fifty Israels could've fit inside the state of Texas. But this was Ilan Ramon's home. His body sure had a long way to go before making it back.

Day eight: Rona—it is so beautiful up here, Ilan Ramon had written to his wife. *The view of Jerusalem from space is magnificent. I can see the Dead Sea. I can see Israel. I know you are down there, somewhere.*

In faded handwriting, it read—*Sometimes, I believe I can even feel you looking up at me. Can you feel me looking down upon you?*

Most of the shuttle had landed out in Hemphill, but there were reports of vehicle fragments falling all throughout east Texas. Littlefield. Newton. Fort Polk. Even Louisiana and parts of Arkansas had reported pieces of debris. Over two thousand crash sites had cropped up over twenty-eight thousand square miles. Thirty-three counties in Texas alone. I remember stepping into our front yard, lured outside by the sound of smashing glass. The windshield of my older brother's Plymouth was completely shattered. Some steaming piece of metal had impaled the passenger-side seat. I could hear the impact of shuttle fragments hitting the roof of our house. Cylinders three feet wide. Loose tubing. A hailstorm of partly charred screws and bolts. It was raining metal everywhere.

Two months have passed since the accident and I've ended up wetting my bed twice. Not all that often in the grand scheme of things, but it's enough to get Mom worried about me. Still having the same nightmare. I'm piloting the *Columbia* now. We're some forty-five miles above the ground. We're coming in for a landing at over sixteen thousand miles per hour. As soon as we cross over the California coast, the orbiter pitches up forty degrees. Temperature sensors are suddenly shutting down. I'm losing control. I perform a roll left to counterbalance the turbulence. The shuttle's showering pieces of debris clear across the country before we

burst into a ball of fire just above Palo Pinto County. But instead of
incinerating with the ship, my body's suddenly in a free fall. I can
see my house just below me, coming up fast. The air surrounding
me brightens. This luminescent trail of superheated gas branches
out in my wake, like I'm a Fourth of July sparkler getting waved
through the air really fast. I am wrapped in that ghastly plasma
that had enveloped the *Columbia* as it plowed through the earth's
atmosphere, a full-body halo of electrically charged particles burning at over three thousand degrees. I'm only seconds away from
punching right through the roof of our house—but whenever I
open my mouth to yell for help, all I can hear coming out from
me is the transmission of static from the *Columbia*'s radio receiver. There's nothing but dead air in my ears anymore, that crackle
crashing against my temples every time I wake up.

Folks are still finding bits of the *Columbia*, even months later.
These scraps of partially buried metal will catch the sunlight,
glimmering up from the dust. Most kids around here have their
own piece of spaceship, even though we were all told "anyone in
unauthorized possession of debris would be prosecuted to the full-
est degree of the law." Trying to scare us off by saying they may
contain hazardous chemicals better left untouched.

I'd promised Mom I wouldn't go out into the neighboring prairie
without her permission anymore. NASA had cordoned off most
of the field anyhow, calling it a crash site now—even though that
would mean most of the southeastern continental United States
would've been considered off-limits to me, from Palo Pinto County
to the Californian coast.

I came across the first page of Ilan Ramon's diary back at the be-

ginning of April. It was half-buried in the prairie behind our backyard, all wet and crumpled, the loose ends flickering in the wind
like bone-white leaves.

Then I saw another. And another. Looked like someone had
ripped up a notebook and let the pages drift off without them.
Took me two whole days to collect them all, sneaking back into
the pasture and picking up the loose sheets when my mother
wasn't around to tell me I couldn't.

I counted thirty-seven pages when all was said and done. I'm
sure there were more, but the weather and elements must've gotten to them before I could. Some of the paper was burned pretty
bad, their edges all singed. The ink had faded.

How his diary survived at all when most of the Columbia had
disintegrated into thin air is beyond me. There just wasn't any ra-
tional explanation for it. Pretty safe to say that this was a miracle.
A hands-down miracle. Somehow his diary had survived the onboard fire. The extreme heat of the explosion. It survived the free
fall to earth—nothing but flimsy meteorites now, paper-thin, enduring the extreme atmospheric cold as its pages fluttered some
forty miles to the ground. It survived exposure to all sorts of severe weather. Two months of strong winds. Rain. And cold, cold
nights.

Just waiting for someone to discover it out here.

Take it back to Israel.

Take these pages home.

*Day thirteen: Rona—even within zero gravity, I can still feel the
pull back toward earth. Toward you, my love.*

Word spread fast throughout Anderson County that the ghost of

Ilan Ramon had possessed the body of some eleven-year-old boy. Apparently, spiritual possession is a simpler pill to swallow here in small-town Texas. A hell of a lot easier to believe than finding a diary from outer space. For this kid to have such intimate information regarding the launch. Details nobody outside of NASA would have known. Not even NASA. No one other than Ilan Ramon himself could've seen these things in orbit.

Wasn't long before NASA was knocking on our door. I decided to come clean about the diary, handing it over. I even showed them where I'd found it, leading the men in black through the prairie. Mom made me apologize for not returning the diary sooner, a bit pissed at me for fibbing in the first place—but I needed to read it for myself.

I needed to see outer space.

I'm not saying I'm the best translator of Hebrew here, but this was about as close to the cosmos as I was ever going to get.

Day fifteen: Only one more day left, Rona, Ilan Ramon had written in his final entry. *One more day and I will be returning home to you.*

That night, Mom kissed me on the forehead before switching off the lights.

The ceiling disappeared. The walls all washed away.

Suddenly I was surrounded by stars.

Good night, Grady, she said before closing the door behind herself. *Sleep tight, baby* . . .

I lay awake, just looking into space, thinking about Ramon still up there, somewhere. From the corner of my eye, I saw one of my glow-in-the-dark star stickers slip off the ceiling. It must've lost its stickiness, drifting to the floor.

A shooting star, right here in my bedroom.

Ilan Ramon had logged fifteen days, twenty-two hours, and twenty minutes in outer space. Beneath that limitless glow-in-the-dark galaxy, I went ahead and prayed for his safe return home. *And it was evening, and it was morning of the sixth day,* as it says in the kiddush, *and creation of heaven and earth were completed with all of their array. Blessed are You, Holy Master, our G-d, King of the Universe, Who creates the fruit of the vine. Blessed are You, Holy Master, our G-d, King of the Universe . . .*

Cropduster

An elderly man drove several blocks through a crowded farmers market Wednesday afternoon, killing nine people and injuring up to 45 pedestrians, 14 critically.

—Fox News, 2003

seven years old

That crop duster kept climbing. Couldn't imagine it flying any higher, but up it went. The pilot aligned his plane with the clouds before flipping upside down, end-over-end, performing this barrel roll that got the audience gasping in the stands.

Ray Winston had rented out a couple acres' worth of his cornfield for the weekend, freshly flattened from the harvest. Folks parked their cars along the highway, the ditches lined up with automobiles for miles. Gates opened early, a couple hours before flying was scheduled to begin, giving spectators a chance to wander about the field. They stepped over the stray cornstalks still matted to the ground, marveling at each plane displayed alongside one another. Close enough to touch.

The P-38 Lightning. The P-40 Warhawk. The T-6 Texan. Even

the Boeing Stearman, right out of Wichita, Kansas. Its upper wings were staggered from the lower, minimizing any aerodynamic interference. I ran my finger down the length of its wooden propeller, rubbing my thumb along the grain. Got this splinter that I carried in my skin for the rest of the day, holding onto it as if the wood were a memento.

My seat had been too big for me. Feet couldn't reach the bleachers below, leaving my legs swinging. I'm sitting in the stands with the rest of town, every neck cricked back. All eyes in the sky. We're watching the planes weave through the air, expelling sentences written in smoke:

WELCOME TO THE AIR SHOW. PICK UP MURRAY'S SUPERIOR POMADE.

Car-to-plane routines. Daredevil stunts. Parachute jumps. Saw this Cessna 152 Aerobat dump some skydiver into the air at three thousand feet. He opens his chute, setting sail—then he releases the clasps and slips out from the harness, free-falling all over again, opening up a second chute before hitting the ground.

But the crop duster was my favorite. Something that fragile, that delicate, taking flight. Here's this dragonfly fluttering just above my head, its paper-thin wings nearly translucent from where I'm sitting. Sunlight seeped through that fabric canvas, illuminating the aluminum struts just underneath, like veins lacing its wings, a symmetrical pattern of brackets holding the airfoil in place.

Felt as if I could grab it. Just reach up and pluck that plane out from the sky. I'd bring my hand back down, cupping that crop duster, its wings buzzing within my palm, this dull hum from the engine vibrating against my skin. As I released my fingers, one by one, the plane would rest on my wrist for a moment before slipping off and ascending into the air all over again.

The pilot had pointed the propeller straight up, maneuvering into another loop-de-loop. All of a sudden, one of its wings started to wobble. Looked as if a bracket had come loose. I'm wondering if I squeezed too hard, accidentally crushing the crop duster in my hand. We all watched its forewing snap back against the plane's broadside, sending the rest of itself into a nosedive. Now it's spiraling through the air. The audience all choked. The air was collectively caught within our lungs as we watched the pilot jump out from the cockpit, a pupa emerging from its cocoon too soon, forced into flight before its wings even had a chance to mature, all wet and tender, free-falling through the air. His hands kept scrambling for the right cord, attempting to yank open his parachute. It quickly slithered out from his back, shriveled and spindly, flapping about, billowing in the wind, unable to catch hold of the air.

The audience all stood within the last five hundred feet, rising up from the bleachers. The pilot's arms kept clawing at the air. Suddenly you can see him reaching out, holding his hands in front of his face, attempting to protect his eyes from the wind shear. As if it burned to look down. The wind's picking up, sounding shrill, hissing all around the crop duster as it crashed into the field first, its wings collapsing into themselves just a few yards off from the stands.

One woman looked away, turning into her husband's shoulder.

Don't look, Thomas, my father said, holding his hands over my eyes. I could feel the sweat in his palms against my eyelids, all warm. But to blink now would be to miss impact. One flinch and it'd all be over.

There was a simple puff of dust. Several people in the audience screamed.

The parachute finally caught a stray draft along the ground, lifting the flimsy membrane of fabric. It's still tethered to the dead pilot. The cords tangled into his limbs, awkwardly bent, as if they were trying to fly away without him.

Where was the line that divided the feat from the accident? I thought this was all a part of the routine. What the audience was watching had been just another stunt, devised to get the crowd gasping. Performed to perfection. I couldn't understand why the pilot never got back up onto his feet again and dust himself off.

Why didn't he wave to the crowd in the stands, all of us suddenly erupting into applause?

thirteen years old

Dad had to ask our neighbor if he could drive him down to the cornfield. He had to wake Mr. McPherson up in the middle of the night. I recognized his car as soon as it pulled off the road, lit in sulfur. The flares lining up along the highway illuminated everything within this rosy glow. The cornstalks, bristling in the wind. The squad car. The asphalt underneath my feet. All pink.

An officer had wrapped me up in a blanket, hanging it over my shoulders to keep me warm. The second I saw my father step out from Mr. McPherson's car, I tried ducking under the covers, like I was in bed back at home, hiding from some bogeyman crawling out of my closet. I could count to ten and he'd be gone, just like that. Nothing but some figment of my imagination. Just some bad dream.

Dad took one look at the fractured fence posts, the length of bent cornstalks leading deeper into the field—and further in, all the way back, the persistent blink of a turn signal, the pulse coming from a familiar tail fin, flashing at the rate of my heartbeat, pounding on and off, on and off.

A bogeyman sure would've been better than my dad right about then.

The market took a dive back in '38. Dipped far enough down that Dad had to sell off his LaSalle. Never remembered seeing him mope around our home as much as the day he had to let go of that car. Acted like a bird with his wings clipped, flapping haplessly through the house all afternoon. Going nowhere.

Wasn't until the fall of '39, when the economy bounced back, that I'm walking home from school and I find a brand-new Cadillac 8-cylinder, fresh off the assembly line, parked right there in our driveway. Prow-shaped radiator, headlamp flanking each side. Looked more like a fighter plane on four wheels.

The Sixty Special.

Five more horses than the '35 V-8. Die-cast grille, fine-pitch bars looking so silver, you could catch your reflection spreading across it.

Most beautiful thing I'd ever seen. I'd sneak out into our garage once I knew Dad had fallen asleep, slipping behind the wheel as soon as I heard him snoring. My feet couldn't reach the pedals below, leaving my legs swinging. There were about three inches in between the tips of my toes and the gas—so I'd tie a pair of tin cans onto my shoes, one under each heel. Stuffed a phone book behind my back for extra leverage, making it easier for me to grip the wheel.

Ten and two.

Time to fly.

Here I am, sitting in the cockpit of a P-38 Lightning, my own high-altitude interceptor. I'm hitting four hundred miles per hour at over twenty thousand feet, shooting down Japanese flying boats in the northern Pacific. I'm holding onto that steering wheel like I'm aiming a .50-caliber machine gun at our neighbor's cat.

Brapt-tat-tat.

Direct hit! Tabby's going down.

Brapt-rat-tat.

Dad had left the keys in the ignition one night. Found them dangling down, swinging back and forth, as if the Cadillac were trying to hypnotize me.

Like it wanted me to take it for a spin.

Come on, Thomas, the dashboard begged. *Just a quick drive around the block.*

I'm on the highway, racing alongside Ray Winston's cornfields. Nothing but this blur of deep green now. The speedometer's flickering at sixty miles an hour. The gauge stands as tall and upright as the cornstalks just outside the window. I could lean in closer to the dashboard and blow the arrow over, pushing it forward another five miles faster—like I'm flying behind enemy lines, below radar, hovering just above the field, the wind off my wings sending every stalk tilting over.

There's this bend in the highway that I must not've seen coming. It's there and then suddenly it isn't.

Now there's no road at all.

The highway yanks the asphalt right out from under me, as if it were practicing that magic trick where you try whipping a tablecloth off the table, keeping all the utensils and plates in place—but I keep driving, hitting Ray Winston's fence at over seventy miles an hour. The posts shatter against the front hood. I'm trying to regain control of the wheel, make a safe landing. But the car keeps plowing through the field. All I can do is watch the stalks divide around me, splitting straight down the middle. There's nothing but green now. Green, everywhere. The headlights are full of it. I can't see beyond the cornstalks brushing up against the fender. I'm listening to the rustle and scrape of leaves and reeds against the Cadillac's underbelly. Each ear of corn makes a hollow *rat-tat-tat* sound whenever it hits metal, as if the car's suddenly under heavy fire.

We've been hit! We're going down . . .

I left Dad's Cadillac in the field. I stumbled back to the highway along the fresh path I just paved through the corn. I could still hear the *click, click* of the car's turn signal, eventually blending in with the crickets chirping away. Fireflies were flashing all around me, like traffic lights shifting through the sky. Telling me to *slow down, stop. Slow down, stop.*

Right before I reached the road—I saw it.

There it was, flitting just above the field. A crop duster drifting over my head, laying down a blanket of pesticide across the corn in the early morn.

And suddenly it all went silent. Nothing but the hum of the plane's engine, buzzing by.

eighty-six years old

Her body rolled over the windshield. Just spun across the hood and up past the glass, this brunette blur twirling into the air. She was gone before my foot could even find the brakes.

She had a peach in her hand. Picked it up from the fruit stand, rubbing her thumb over the fuzz to feel for bruises—now she was carrying it across the car, unable to let go, crushing it within her fist. She'd held out her hand before her face, to protect herself, her palm pressing against the windshield. The peach imploded like a bug smashing against the glass. Pulp running down her wrist now. Dribbling down the window.

We made eye contact. This quick glimpse, where I see her and she sees me. Her eyes are wide, misunderstanding. Not scared. Just confused. Puzzled, as if she couldn't figure out what was happening all around her. What any of this was. As if she were about to ask me through the windshield—*What's going on, Thomas? What are you doing?*

But everything's moving so fast. It's happening all at once. There's no time to answer. Her head rotates away with the rest of her body, shoulder over shoulder, before swiveling back around, our eyes locking onto each other's once more, the two of us discovering one another all over again.

She had blue eyes.

Her shoulder rebounded off the roof, her body spinning into the air. When all I wanted was to stop.

Stop time.

Stop the car.

Stop all of this.

The traffic lights had kept shifting just outside the windshield, like fireflies flashing through the sky. One second, they're just a few yards ahead of the car—the next, they're blocks away. I can't seem to see where the intersection ends anymore. Only to disappear completely. Where the road went, I couldn't say—but it's not in front of me anymore. It's a thicket. I'm in a field. There's no seeing three feet in front of me, the brush is so high. The fender parts through, splitting the tall grass straight down the middle. There are vegetables everywhere. Corn rolls over the windshield. Tomatoes splat against the glass.

I hit the accelerator, thinking it's the brakes. Just a tap on the gas. That pressure under the heel—and suddenly, there's a heave in speed. The arrow on the speedometer flickers back and forth, quivering as if a wind just blew through the field, pressing the cornstalks down. I hear the soft rustle of brush scraping below the underbelly of my Buick—unaware that I'm actually listening to pedestrians passing underneath me, their bodies. It's not a sound I'm able to understand just yet, manslaughter of some type.

Then I see her. She turns toward the car just in time for her knees to meet the fender. She holds her hands out ahead of herself, barricading herself behind her palms. Presenting her peach to me.

I've lost control of time. Once second it's ten twenty.

The next it's nine fifteen.

I can't seem to get a grip of what hour it is. Hand over hand, I'm climbing up the clock—grabbing hold of the steering wheel and trying to turn back time.

Ten and two. Nine and three. Keep your hands on the wheel at all times.

Where this farmer's market came from . . . Why today these three blocks were closed off to traffic, no matter how many times I've driven down this very street.

Why they took the road away from me today.

I'll never know.

The windshield cracked without shattering, right where the woman's head first met the glass. For a moment, I thought I must have passed out—long enough for a spider to spin a web just over my head, wrapped up in a mesh of fractured glass. My chest is hanging low, shoulders drooping over.

I'm done struggling with this car. I have to use the steering wheel just to hold myself up. I look out my window to see all the collapsed tents, the bent metal frames. Fruit strewn all over the sidewalk.

My door suddenly opens from the outside. Some man's hand grabs hold of my shoulder. He starts yelling at me as another pair of hands grab me by the arm. Someone else is trying to pry my own hands free from the steering wheel.

But I don't want to let go.

I can't.

I was simply picking up groceries for me and my wife, you see. She's expecting me home any minute now. More men crowd around the outside of the car, all of them reaching in—while I just hold onto the wheel, begging them to let me go. *Please don't take my license away. I've been driving my whole life. I can't remember a time when I wasn't behind the wheel.* When enough of them have a good grip, they pull me out. A pupa emerging from its cocoon too soon.

They lifted me up above everyone else, holding me in the air. Carrying me over the loose shoes, the crushed fruit.

Flying.

buffet of the damned

While the ill passengers aboard the Royal Caribbean ship haven't been officially diagnosed yet, according to the Centers for Disease Control (CDC), the 577 passengers and 49 crew members who are sick to their stomachs, vomiting and experiencing diarrhea are likely infected with norovirus.

—*TIME* MAGAZINE, 2014

The breakfast buffet truly was a thing of beauty. An all-you-can-eat Eden, hand to God. We're talking three times the size of any Sizzler I'd ever pulled up a plate at before. Three times, *at least*. Nothing but a temple of steam tables as far as the hungry eye could see . . .

You got vats of scrambled eggs bubbling over in a yolky yellow bog. I half imagined I might pull out a perfectly preserved woolly mammoth with my serving tongs, like I was eating at the snack bar back at the La Brea Tar Pits.

You got a whole hog's worth of sausage links stacked over a dozen high. Reminded me of that chapel of bones they built in Rome me and Margie visited on our honeymoon.

And pyramids of pastries tastier than anything the Egyptians ever erected!

This was gonna be a two-plate affair, I swear . . .

Margie hadn't even reached the turf portion of the surf-and-turf table and already there was an avalanche of popcorn shrimp toppling off her dish.

Pace yourself, hon, I say. *They don't shut the buffet down till eleven . . .*

Our own little Billy was manning the waffle station like he'd been hired by the cruise line to whip up waffles for all the other passengers. Taking their orders and everything—*You want chocolate chips in yours, sir? How about bananas, ma'am?*

Sally swore up and down she's on a diet—though this was the first I'd heard word of it. There were some boys onboard who'd caught her eye, so I'm thinking this was her way of prepping to put on that bikini I didn't approve of. Not one bit.

You gotta eat something, Sally, Margie says. *At least take a bacon or two.*

Sally's been huffing and puffing ever since we boarded the boat, rolling her eyes every chance she gets, like she's embarrassed to be sitting next to her parents.

You believe that? Ashamed of her own flesh and blood!

I said I'm not hungry, Ma, our little girl gripes. *Can I go to the pool now, please?*

You may not, missy, I cut into the conversation, putting my foot down on this disrespectful behavior once and for all. *You're gonna sit here with your parents till these plates are pecked clean and that's that, you hear?*

The deckhands were gonna have to roll us Pendletons out once we were done with this buffet, 'cause you better believe we were all heading back for seconds.

As a *family*.

This was our dream vacation. A ten-day fantasy cruise through the Caribbean. Margie got us a great deal on a package tour through one of those travel websites she's always sneaking a peek at late at night. Thanks to her penny-pinching, the Pendleton clan has traveled far and wide. You name it—African safaris, visits to the Great Wall of China, backpacking through the moors of Scotland.

But never a tropical getaway on board a four-star luxury cruise liner, no sir.

Think it's pretty safe to say I've never set foot on anything quite like the *Argonautica* before. Over nine hundred feet long. Fourteen decks altogether. A regular floating palace. This ship's just about got something for the whole family. Four pools. That's one pool per Pendleton! Not to mention the fine dining. We could eat at a different restaurant every evening, if we wanted. How about a spa for the ladies? A mini-golf course for the kids. A Broadway musical revue. Karaoke. An arcade. Even a casino!

It takes a crew of eight hundred to look after all three thousand passengers, treating each and every one of us like we were royalty. Kings and queens o' the sea.

You thirsty, sir? Here's a frozen daiquiri right out of the blender.

Hungry, ma'am? How about a shrimp cocktail, chilled on ice.

You never even need to leave the comfort of your own deck chair. The waitstaff brings everything right to you on a silver platter with a smile.

Now how's that for service?

Say you get seasick and have yourself a little accident. Don't you worry over it one bit—'cause here comes auxiliary services swooping in to the rescue, swabbing up that spill faster than any hazmat unit ever will. Like it never even happened.

Out of stomach, out of mind.

Margie's the first to notice the passenger at the neighboring table suddenly looking a little green around the gills. She elbows me to take a look-see—and sure enough, this poor fellow's seeming pretty queasy. Clutching his stomach. Moaning low. Sweating through his silk floral-print shirt, even within the cozy climate control.

I chalked it up to seasickness. Three days out on the briny blue must've done a number on him. Happens to the best of us onboard. But in less than a blink and a belch—*hyuuuurch*—this fellow buckles over and plasters his pancakes in a layer of gravy and reconstituted eggs Benedict. The ick of it just rushes right on over the table. Splashes up against the folks sitting across from him.

Surf's up on the surf and turf . . .

His wife starts sopping up his vomit with her sarong. She's just sponging up as much of the stuff as she can, apologizing profusely to the other passengers at their table for the mess—while this foam-mouthed fellow picks himself up and proceeds to—*hyuuulgh*—puke on the people helping themselves to the creamed chipped beef right behind him.

I'm asking you now—*What's cruise line etiquette in this kind of situation?*

Do you help your fellow man? Or do you turn a blind eye and

pretend it's not happening? 'Cause with over a hundred diners waiting in the buffet line, sure seemed like it was every vacationer for themselves. A stampede of panicked passengers charged straight for the dining hall's exit, hollering their heads off. I watched the slower folks get shoved to the floor by the people behind them.

Women and children first, my foot. Nobody stopped long enough to pick them up, no sir. Trampled right on over.

Let's head for the deck, kids, I say. *How about some fun in the sun?*
One little particle.

That's all it takes.

One infinitesimal fleck of feces finds its way into your food, the tiniest microbe making its way down your mouth—and that's it, *God bless,* you're done. Suddenly your stomach's churning over like a dinghy caught in a rocky tsunami.

The nausea. The vomiting. The diarrhea.

You're one of them now. *A carrier.*

You're infected.

Now just how in the heck's a fellow supposed to protect his family against something like that?

Now they're saying nothing's safe to touch onboard anymore.

Elevator buttons.

Doorknobs.

Handrails.

No amount of hand sanitizer can stop it. Once the pathogen's lipid envelope latches on to your skin, it's only a matter of time before you start showing symptoms. We're talking acute gastroenteritis, abdominal pain, lethargy, muscle aches, headaches, coughing, low-grade fever. The list goes on and on.

Everybody stay together now, I say once we've made our way up to the sundeck. *And don't touch anything.*

Sweet Jesus, Petey, Margie cries. *What's happening here? What's going on?*

Don't you fret, hon. Probably just a bad batch of seafood, I'm sure. Everything's gonna be just fine.

That's when I smell it. Something acidic in the air. One whiff and my nostrils begin to burn. It smells like . . .

. . . *bile.*

I peek at the pool and realize the water has fogged over in these milky pink clouds of regurgitated shrimp cocktail. Clusters of seagulls are pecking away at the puddles of puke accumulating along the promenade. There's chowder everywhere.

I spot a lifeguard wobbling on his feet, shuffling our way.

Oh, thank goodness, I say. *I was beginning to worry we—*

I cut myself off as soon as I noticed the froth around his mouth.

Oh, boy . . .

Sally just starts screaming bloody murder. This bleached blonde must be the boy she's been batting her eyelashes at! The front of his bare bronzed chest is spackled in lumpy chunks of last night's lobster. He's dry-heaving with every step. Sounds like a donkey with colic, hocking up pockets of trapped air from his lungs.

Salllll . . . ly. Salllll . . . ly.

He's rasping out my daughter's name, *my little angel,* acting like he's some kind of infected gentleman caller, reaching out his dripping hand for her to take.

And she's reaching back! You believe that? The nerve of this girl!

Well—you better believe I did what any father faced with a pandemicked suitor would do. I brought my flip-flopped foot right up and gave that Coppertoned kid a good kick in the ribs before he could lay one festering finger on my little girl.

Hands off, mister!

I must've underestimated my own strength, 'cause this lifeguard hits the handrail pretty good and—*whoopsie*—wouldn't you know it, he's upended himself, head over heels, heading right into the drink.

Almost.

I race to the rail just in time to see him splat against the mezzanine three decks below. Pops upon impact like a tick fattened up on too much blood. Most of it splashes over the elderly couple playing shuffleboard right beside his body. The woman pushes her paddle through the expanding pool of his oozing bodily fluids. Nudges that lifeguard's jawbone along for a three-point score.

All right, gang. I rally the troops before Sally can lean over and see what's left of her leaking lifeguard. *Let's, uh—let's all head back to our cabin now.*

I'd say this was all getting out of hand about now.

All heck's breaking loose on the deck. I watched one contaminated passenger rush up to a waiter and release a stream of unidentifiable shellfish straight into his face. It's coming out of him in cascades. Just gushes of it. He's spurting all over the whole promenade, like a water sprinkler that's accidentally been left on—*click, click, click, click, click-click-click, click-click—click, click, click, click, click-click-click* . . .

I've never seen anything like it. And we're not just talking about the passengers anymore, no sir. Even the crew's getting infected now.

The waitstaff. Housecleaning. Guest services. The Broadway dancers.

Nobody's safe onboard.

I'm sure you're wondering, as I was—*Pray tell, where is our trusted captain during this whole hullabaloo?* He'd gotten on the intercom, encouraging passengers to quarantine themselves to their cabins.

The safest place for you is your stateroom, his disembodied voice crackled over the PA system, echoing throughout the whole ship. He announced his decision to turn the boat around and sail back the way we came, cutting our sunny sojourn short by six days. The plan was to dock in New Jersey—still a day or two away.

We apologize for the inconvenience this outbreak of food poisoning has caused our guests . . .

Outbreak, my behind. I don't know what ivory porthole you've been peeking out of, pal, but we're not talking some run-of-the-mill food poisoning here. This wasn't just some case of E. coli. This was *biblical.* Revelations or what have you—*And I saw seven angels having the seven last plagues; for in them is filled up the wrath of God.* This is *exactly* what happens when man lets his opulence get the best of him.

Pestilence on the seven seas.

Until we dock, our captain asked, *please avoid contact with any passengers showing symptoms of illness.*

Easier said than done, sir. That's over seven hundred contaminated passengers and counting. And those numbers were only growing by the day. *The hour.* Another night at sea and—*good morning,* everybody onboard this ship would be infected. By the time we reached the Jersey shore, there wouldn't be anyone left.

Us Pendletons were fighting for our survival here.

What're we gonna do, Petey? Margie asks. *What're we gonna do?!*

Get back to the cabin, I say. *We're gonna batten down the hatches and sit tight till we reach landfall and the Centers for Disease Control can save us. Got that, kids?*

Our cabin was located on deck seven. The residential floors were nothing but a maze of hallways clamoring with puking passengers.

Don't stop for anybody, you hear? I shouted over my shoulder to the rest of the fam. *No matter who it is or how much they beg, you just keep running—okay?*

Wherever I stepped, there was a slight *squish* beneath my feet. I felt a wetness sop through my flip-flops, seeping in between my toes, like I was walking through the marshlands or the like. I looked down and noticed the nautical-themed carpeting was now covered in a splatter pattern of crab legs and fruit cocktail. The walls were dripping wet with what looked like fresh Jackson Pollock paintings.

Almost there! Just keep running, kids! Eyes on the prize now!

Room 237! Home at last . . .

I swipe my key card.

Nothing. The light doesn't turn green.

Come on, come on, come on . . .

The card's a bit slippery, slickened up with something or other, so it takes a couple swipes before—

Open sez-a-me!

The bolt mechanically unlatches with a hollow *thwonk*. I open the door for Margie. *Ladies first.* She's looking pretty pale. Perspiration's pebbling her temples.

Margaret? You okay, hon?

Oh. You know. I'm not feeling so swift . . .

She's got it.

A little voice in the back of my head pipes up—*Your wife's caught it.* Sounds like someone whispering into my ear—*Margaret's sick.*

I push her.

May the Lord have mercy on my soul, I shoved my own wife, the mother of my children, inside our cabin and slammed the door on her, sealing her in.

Petey . . . ? She calls out. *Petey, what's going on?*

You just, uh—why don't you just take a nap? Okay, hon? Me and the kids are gonna—we're gonna head to the mezzanine and let you rest for a spell. Okay?

There's silence from the other side of the door. I lean in and press my ear to the paneling.

Honey . . . ? I can hear her breathing. Her lungs sound wet.

Protect the kids, she finally says, her voice seeping through. *Whatever you do, Peter Pendleton, you promise me you'll keep them safe.*

I look back to Billy and Sally. *I will, Margaret.*

Swear to me, Petey . . . Swear on your life!

I swear! God help me, I swear.

That's when Sally screams right in my ear. I turn to discover another passenger plowing down the hall, running right for us. The panic's thick on his face. If I was a betting man, from the look in his eyes, I'd say he was making a beeline to the closest commode— only it's just dawning on him that he isn't gonna make it.

Run, I say. *Run!*

It's too late. This man's pulling down his pants, pleading with us.

Ruuuuuun!

Billy trips. I stop and pick him up by the scruff of his neck and throw him as hard as I can down the hall before he can get wet.

Goooooo!

I've got no choice but to fall on this gastrointestinal grenade, using my body to absorb as much of the explosion as I can before it hits the kids. I can feel the warmth—anal napalm—as it seeps into my Hawaiian shirt. I know it's only a matter of seconds before I'm done for.

I strip down to my civvies and pray there aren't any open cuts along my body.

There! Down the hall! I spot a housecleaning cart. Tucked under the dirty linen hamper is a rack of heavy-duty industrial cleaning agents.

No time to waste. Gotta to act fast.

I grab the first bottle of liquid bleach I can find. Popping the top with my teeth, I take a deep breath and pour that chlorine-based chemical solution all over.

Take that, you dumb bug! Let's see you survive this rinse!

It burns all right. Oh, boy—does it burn. I can feel the singe in my skin, like there's too much chlorine in the pool. I can feel it in my lungs. It burns to even breathe. It's a bit blurry around the edges of my eyes.

Then suddenly everything goes white.

I'm flying a bit blind now.

You okay, Dad? Little Billy asks, taking my hand and leading me down the hall.

I'm all right. I'm all right . . . Let's just get your dad above deck, okay? I think some fresh air would do me some good right about now.

Hard to tell if I'm wincing from the sun or if the bleach has eaten my retinas right out. Either which way, it takes a moment for my eyes to adjust to see what's happening all around us. And when they do, I'm not so sure I ever want to see again.

We're surrounded.

The whole deck's chock-full of a swarming horde, stumbling along the promenade. Mouths frothing with vomit. Some are going about their vacation like nothing's changed. Slipping and sliding over the shuffleboard court. Putt-Putting through the puddles.

There were some survivors. Not many. I could spot pockets of passengers fighting for their lives here and there.

I watched one newlywed couple take each other's hands and jump overboard.

And the band played on, the brass section filtering even streams of vomit across the deck, puddles pooling up at their feet.

I'm scared, Daddy, Sally says to me, our backs now pressed against the handrail as the multitude of stained vacationers starts to wander aimlessly our way.

Don't be, I say, trying hard not to sound so scared myself. *Come here. Both of you kids. Huddle up with your father for a second.*

Sally and Billy each took a knee next to me. I wrapped my arms

around their shoulders for a little impromptu Pendleton pow-
wow—*Who are we?*

The Pendletons.

That's right. And what do the Pendletons always do?

Stick together, no matter what.

Exactly, I say, choking up. *A Pendleton never abandons their family. We stick together. So listen up, you two. No matter what happens,
I want you to know—I love you. Your mother loves you. We will be
with you forever and ever. So just close your eyes and think about how
much your parents love you and this will all be over soon.*

The seagulls are swarming over our heads as the sun sets right
behind us. I take in a deep breath, getting a good lungful of that
salty sea air.

And right before we're about to leap overboard . . .

I'm reminded of our first night on this dream cruise. Me and
Margaret had snuck off, leaving the kids in the arcade for some
romantic one-on-one time. Just the two of us. *Isn't this just the life,
Margaret?* I ask in between sips of my daiquiri, taking in that love-
ly sunset, the entire horizon as pink as an undercooked slice of
sirloin.

Think I've died and gone straight to heaven, she says, nuzzling
her head into the nape of my neck. *I never wanna go home again.*

*Well—to heck with Hennepin County, then. This boat's our new
home now.*

Oh, Petey . . . You're such a kidder.

I love you, Margaret Pendleton.

I love you, hon.

I open my eyes—and I'm brought back onboard the boat.

To brave little Billy.

To my sweet Sally.

I'm a Pendleton, all right—and a Pendleton never abandons his family. We can't let this ship reach dry land. If we dock, this outbreak will spread—and spread *fast*. First, Jersey. New York'll be next. Then the rest of America right behind it. How long before the whole globe's brought to its knees before the porcelain alter?

Somebody's gotta keep the *Argonautica* from docking at all costs. Somebody's gotta get to the bridge and take control of this ship before it's too late.

Somebody's gotta save the world.

Might as well be the Pendletons.

mouth-to-mouth

She looked like she was sleeping. Completely peaceful. If I'd just stumbled on her I would've had zero problems believing she was simply taking a nap. Resting on her back, like that. Eyes closed. The faintest trace of a smile tugging on her lips—like she was simply adrift in a dream, you know? Lost in La La Land.

I even caught myself wondering what she was dreaming about . . .

Focus. I had to focus. I was losing her. Her pale nectarine cheeks had a sheen to them already, shining under the fluorescent lights. I leaned over and pressed my mouth against hers. Her lips were cold—soft plastic—like a pair of thin sponges.

You're not proposing to her, Pendleton, Mr. Powers grumbled over my shoulder. *Get in there and save her life.*

Someone snickered behind me. Sounded like Craig Teasdale. *That* asshole.

Focus. I had to focus. Stop harping on her looks so much. I was losing her. Time was running out. The clock kept ticking in my ear, chiseling at my concentration. Forty-seven seconds had already slipped past—*forty-eight, forty-nine, fifty*—and I hadn't even started CPR yet. She'd gone into respiratory arrest over a minute ago. Thoracic movements were long gone.

It was up to me to save her. To usher the oxygen back inside her lungs.

I was in our school's marching band. We're talking first tuba here. If anyone could revive this girl, it was bound to be me. I'd forced my breath through tougher ducts than this. Puckering up to my mouthpiece for the last five years, I'd say, had granted me something of a home-court advantage for this particular predicament.

So let's do this. I mouthed out every step below my breath as I went:

Tilt the head back. Lift the chin. Pinch the nose. Cover the mouth with your own and release the oxygen from your lungs until you see their chest visibly rise.

Still no response.

I couldn't pick up a pulse. Shouldn't she have a pulse? Her eyes kept closed, sealed off from me, that half-smile still on her lips— her mind lost in some idyllic thought. She looked so peaceful. *Beautiful.* The free-throw circle wreathed her head like some kind of a halo, like the entire basketball court was all a part of some Italian fresco and she was St. Teresa of Avila in the throes of ecstasy or whatever.

Focus. I had to focus.

Press the heel of your hands, one on top of the other, against the center of the rib cage. Lock your elbows. Depress the chest two inches deep.

Pump hard and fast, thirty full thrusts before administering oxygen once more.

Pump and blow.

Pump and blow.

Pump and blow.

I brought my ear to her lips, listening for an exhale. Once her rubber lung deflated, the membrane in the non-breathing valve was supposed to close the passage to the inspiration tube. From there, the air should've been redirected toward the exhaust portal. Whatever breath I'd forced into her mouth cavity should funnel out again, my own recycled air poofing out as if she were gasping back to life. Her eyes would bolt open and lock onto mine—some total stranger hovering above her, kneeling just next to her head, staring down at her like a complete moron.

Her hero. Her knight in shining gym shorts.

Hey, I'd say. *How's it going? I just saved your life. No big deal . . .*

The whole class was on their knees, each student stooping over their own mannequin. I spotted Craig slipping his the tongue, groping at her foamy breasts.

Quit it, Teasdale, Mr. Powers barked from the sidelines. *This is not prom.*

Check out the hot girl-on-girl action going on, Craig announced to our female classmates locking lips with their mannequins. *Somebody oughta be filming this . . .*

One more crack like that and you can pay a visit to the principal, Mr. Powers droned, bored with us already. You could totally tell he'd rather be running basketball drills than slog through yet another year of CPR. Can't say I blamed him.

Glancing around the gym, I noticed everybody's mannequin looked exactly alike. Same modular construction, same foam-molded soft plastic. Even that placid expression sculpted on their faces was completely identical. Over a dozen indistinguishable gaping mouths, desperate for air. Our class was using the basic torso model—circa, like, twenty years ago. We're talking a woman's trunk here, not much else. Both arms were severed at the shoulders like on that alabaster statue of the Venus de Milo. Beyond a fastening bolt for optional body parts, "sold separately," everything else was missing. She was just a head, a mouth, and some obstructed lungs.

Her name was Suzanne.

Rescue Suzanne.

It's not like each mannequin had a different name. Everybody's was named Suzanne. That's what the company called her. Trademarked and everything.

But I caught myself saying her name in between chest compressions—*Come on, Suzanne. Come on. Breathe for me. Breathe.*

She still hadn't responded.

I kept up with the compressions—*one, two, three, breathe, one, two, three, breathe*—but the air seemed to lose itself within the labyrinth of her inflation valves. If her head remained in a neutral position, the inspiration tube would stay locked, simulating a tongue obstruction or a blocked airway or whatever. I had to force the oxygen past the face-coupling mechanism and through the airway connector.

Through the inspiration tube. Through the valve membrane.

Into her lungs.

Come on, Suzanne. Breathe for me. Breathe.

I pressed my lips firmly against hers and exhaled again. I

should've known it was only my own body heat seeping into the soft plastic—but for a moment, just this lamebrained second, I hesitated, yanking my head back and staring down at her.

Her lips felt warm. Warmer than before.

I could've sworn they even looked pink.

Flushed.

I leaned over her mouth and listened in, straining to hear her exhale. My ear grazed against her lips, just slightly. I tried to block out the sound of the other students, clear the whole class from my mind until it was only Suzanne and me.

Breathe, Suzanne. Breathe . . .

Then I heard it. The faintest exhale drifted out from her mouth-piece.

Breath.

Warm breath rushed over my ear.

I had to wait until my lunch period to sneak back into the gym. It's not like I sit with anybody in the cafeteria anyway, so this wasn't *Mission: Impossible* or anything. I just waltzed out. Mr. Powers keeps the CPR mannequins in the athletic supply closet amongst all the track and field equipment. I had volunteered to pack them up after class was over, so—*oops*—guess who left the padlock unlatched?

All the Suzannes were stored in their own soft-pack carrying cases. I quickly unzipped hers, pulling off the head-protection box and resting her on the floor.

Suzanne just stared at the ceiling. She didn't actually have eyes. Just smooth plastic cupolas over each socket where they should've been. Nothing but foamy domes, always closed. Her mouth still hung open, grinning a bit. Was she dreaming? Maybe.

I felt like I should say something. To her. But . . . what? What's there to say?

Hi . . . ? What's up . . . ?

So I went through the CPR steps again. Slowly this time. *Gently.* Savoring each phase. No rushing.

I checked Suzanne for responsiveness, pressing my fingers to her neck.

No pulse. No breath.

I rested my hands against the center of her chest and pushed down. Firm this time. *Rhythmically.* The marching band had been learning Bon Jovi's "You Give Love a Bad Name" for Friday's big game. The tuba line had plenty of tempo. I paced my chest compressions to the chromatic scale—*two, three, four, two, three, four . . .*

I wasn't gonna lose her.

I tilted her head back. Lifted her chin. Pinched her nose and brought my lips to her mouth and emptied the air from my lungs. I gave her all the oxygen I had.

My breath was hers.

A rush of water erupted from her mouth. It was warm from her body, stuck in her lungs. I couldn't duck in time, getting an eyeful. Even swallowed some. There was this briny taste to it—brackish river water. Where the funk did that come from?

Suzanne kept coughing. Each breath sounded wet.

Are you—are you okay? Are you cold?

She was shivering. She wasn't wearing anything, her torso totally exposed—and here I am, just gaping at her like an idiot. I'd spent all of third period pressing my hands against her boobs. The least I could do was put some clothes on her.

Here. Put this on . . .

I gave her my hoodie, covering her up. She didn't have any arms, so I just kind of draped it over her shoulders, tying off the sleeves around her neck.

My name's William . . . Billy, if you want. Either's fine.

We just sat there, not talking. The rasp from her lungs echoed through the basketball court, her breathing slowly balancing itself out again.

I had a hard time figuring out what to do with my hands. Where to put them. In my pockets? On my lap? Just let them hang out at my sides?

She whispered something. I couldn't catch it.

What was that? I leaned over to listen. *Say that again?*

L'Inconnue de la Seine . . .

Okay. I know how this all sounds.

One of the school's CPR training mannequins suddenly goes missing.

That's bad.

Then it comes out a student stole it.

That's *really* bad.

But Suzanne wasn't just some doll. It took some Internetting, but I sleuthed it all out. Here's her story: Somewhere in the 1880s, the body of an unidentified girl gets pulled out of the Seine river in Paris. Police automatically suspect suicide, considering there were no marks, no cuts, no bruises on her body.

Just a pretty face. A placid smile. Closed eyes.

L' Inconnue de la Seine, they called her.

I've been failing French for like forever now, so when she first said it, it took me a moment to translate—"The unknown woman from the Seine."

She couldn't have been any older than sixteen. The pathologist responsible for her body was "so taken by her looks," he made this wax plaster-cast death mask of her face. Like you did in those days, you know? But that death mask totally blew up. As in, copies of her face were being reproduced all through Paris. You could find her mask adorning the mantels of upper-crust bohemian society everywhere.

Everybody wanted her.

Wanted to look like her.

Girls modeled their looks off her. Trying to imitate that half-smile. She was the most beautiful woman in all of France . . . So when some Swedish medical-supply company needed a model for its resuscitation mannequins—they settled on her.

Her face became the template for Rescue Suzanne. Every time some high schooler plants their lips on one of those CPR dolls, it's her they're kissing.

I revived her. I saved her life.

Hearing her say my name—*Beellee*—nobody says my name like that.

What is this place, Beellee?

Where are my arms, Beellee?

What has happened to me, Beellee?

I'm surprised Mademoiselle Davidson didn't realize I was much more fluent in French now, thanks to Suzanne. She was a much better teacher. It took me a while to get the hang of it, but now I'm tossing out past participles and verb tenses like the best of those AP Frenchies. Suck on that.

Waiting until phys ed to see her was the worst part. Twenty-four hours had to go to by before I could find her—and even then, it had to be under the pretense of our CPR unit. Do you know how hard it was to make sure I had the exact same Suzanne mannequin every time? Considering they all look the same, I had to figure out how to set her apart from the rest—so I took a Sharpie and gave her a little birthmark. Nothing anyone else would notice. Just a little Marilyn Monroe mole above her lip.

But even then, I had to try and act all nonchalant about singling her out from the others. I nearly blew my cover once when Craig grabbed my Suzanne before I could. You better believe I wasn't going to sit back and watch that asshole grope her all through class. I grabbed her back before he could manhandle her anymore.

Chill out, fag, Craig said. *Get your own fuck-doll . . .*

This wasn't about sex. I'm serious.

I can't explain it, but—of all the thousands of manufactured dolls, somehow, it was my mannequin—*my Suzanne*—that was possessed by the ghost of the girl whose lungs were forever overwhelmed with water over a hundred years ago.

Out of all the mannequins she could've inhabited, she haunted mine.

She came to *me*.

I started imagining all the different kids who'd kissed her in class. We had third period together—but what about first and second? Fourth and fifth? At the beginning of each class, Mr. Powers would hand each student their own hygienic face shield—just some Saran Wrap dental dam to keep us from spreading herpes amongst the student body or whatever. At the end of the day, Mr. Powers would peel back each mannequin's face and dump the skin in some sanitizing solution, letting their lips soak overnight so they'd be completely disinfected by the next day. I had volunteered to help once—only to watch Mr. Powers scalp Suzanne with his bare hands, yanking off her face. All that was left were the tubes and mouth mechanisms.

Nothing but a plastic skull.

I had to get Suzanne out of school.

I had to get her home.

Band practice was after school. It was easy enough to slip her inside my tuba's gig bag. She fit perfectly. It was a soft case, so you couldn't tell. We walked out the front door, Suzanne strapped to my back. Nobody even gave us a second glance.

We were free.

Where are we, Beellee? What is this—this Green Day?

Why do you hide me under your bed, Beellee?

Where do you go all day, Beellee?

Why did you leave me, Beellee?

I went ahead and ordered her other body parts directly from

the company's website. They had everything. Soft lower body. Arms and legs. You could even order accessories. Replaceable chest skin. Molded hairpieces. Additional lung plates and sternum springs. Cleaned out my bank account, but it was worth it. *She* was worth it.

Suzanne would be happier now. She'd feel complete.

The website also offered a bland blue jacket-and-trouser set, but I preferred pulling out a summer dress from my sister's closest. Silk. Yellow and pink flowers. Spaghetti straps and a wrapped V-neck. Sis didn't even notice it was missing.

I did the eyes. I just took a Sharpie and inked them in the best I could. I'm no artist, I know. Her left eye is a little larger than the right. She's kinda cross-eyed.

But she can look at me now. For the longest time, it was like staring into a pair of peaches. Just smooth, shiny plastic. No eyeballs, no eyebrows, no eyelashes.

Now she can see.

See me.

Why is there metal wrapped around your teeth, Beellee?

Why do you look at me that way, Beellee? Why do you look so sad, Beellee?

When can I go outside, Beellee?

The first time we kissed in a non–cardiopulmonary resuscitation kinda way, I realized like, right off how awkward it was. We were in my room, on my bed. It was late. My parents were asleep. I'd put on some music. We'd been talking for hours and then suddenly there was this lull in the conversation—so I did what any guy in that situation would do. I closed my eyes and leaned in.

But as soon as my lips pressed against Suzanne's, I realized there was totally no give. No opening of her mouth. No tongue. Just the most minimal amount of her lips, like the absolute least amount of kissing compliance she'd have to give and still technically be considered a kiss.

That was like, a week ago now?

I haven't tried since.

Suzanne always talks about Paris. The winding cobblestone streets. The smell of freshly baked bread drifting along the sidewalk. The Seine.

I told her I'd take her back if she really wanted to go—but she got real quiet. Her eyes kinda glazed over, as if she was lost in her thoughts. Her mind went elsewhere for a bit.

That's happening a lot lately. Her mind just drifts. There's no reaching her.

What're you thinking about? She hates it when I ask her that. Starts muttering under her breath in French, like really, *really* fast, saying stuff I can't make out.

So I stopped asking.

I've told her a little about my life—*Living here, you know, it's not like Paris. It's pretty boring, actually. There aren't many places to go, other than the Chesterfield Towne Center or Regency Mall. There's the James River, but it's not like the Seine or anything. A lot of kids from school will drive down there on a Friday night and drink on the flattened rocks that crop up along the river. Some girl in my class actually got really wasted one night and slipped, hitting her head on a rock and tumbling into the water. The currents picked her up and whisked her off. The fire department's river rescue unit fished her body out about half a mile away from where she first fell in . . .*

Suzanne's eyes lit up. I suddenly wondered if I should be telling her this. She'd been quiet the whole time I was yammering, just listening, staring back at me.

Take me, Beellee, she whispered. *Please. Show me . . .*

It was easy to find the spot where the girl had fallen in. The rocks were all spray-painted with her name—RIP MARY BETH, WE LUV YOU, 2 YOUNG 2 GO.

It felt weird being outside with Suzanne. Even late at night, I felt like we were gonna get caught. Some drunk metalhead would be down there, sipping his 40, and he'd see me lugging Suzanne across the rocks and think I was dumping a body.

Suzanne hadn't said much since we'd left the house. The car ride was completely quiet. I kept wanting to say something, but nothing I could think of felt right. But now, out there on the rocks, she whispered to me—*Let me go, Beellee.*

I pretended like I hadn't heard her, so she said it louder—*Let me go back.*

I'd left her arms and legs back at home. It was easier to transport just her torso in my tuba bag—so when I finally eased her body into the water, she bobbed along like a toy boat in the bathtub. I'd placed her on her back. She didn't ask, but I wanted her to be able to stare up at all of the stars in the sky.

Before I could find the courage to say, *Please don't leave me,* Suzanne kissed me on the cheek.

And I let her go. *Merci, Beellee,* she said as she drifted away. *Au revoir . . .*

A jogger spotted her washed up alongside the riverbank on his early-morning run, all covered in mud, and called 911. Her body showed no signs of violence. No cuts or bruises. Most likely a suicide. Even after she had been in the water for hours, getting dragged along by the currents, her lips still held the slightest smile.

reward money

I'm proposing a toast.

To Larissa McKee. Sweetest little girl I ever laid eyes on.

Found her floating facedown in the pool out back. Turned her right over and there was that runny button nose, those sweet dimpled cheeks. One look at those milky white eyes and I knew she was just the gal for me. Changed my life forever.

This round's on her, boys. Better make it last. Her parents aren't paying for the next one.

First night I tried checking in here, the manager wouldn't budge on the price, leaving me four dollars short. *Four lousy bucks.* Wasn't as if he didn't have enough rooms to spare. Half of this damn motel was empty and he still wouldn't let me stay.

Then come the McKees, hefting their luggage into the lobby. You could tell they were tired. Must've been driving all day. Little Larissa could barely keep her eyes open. Nearly passed out on her feet, she was so sleepy, leaning her head against her mother's hip.

Mr. McKee pipes in from behind me, saying—*Excuse me, sir.* He pulls out his wallet and yanks up a fiver, like he's paying some toll. *You can keep the dollar.*

I grab that bill and say *thanks*, snitching the keys to my room. Took one last look at little Larissa before heading out the door, watching her drowsy eyes follow me through the lobby.

Never saw her again.

Not alive, at least.

Her picture started popping up on telephone poles around town. I'd find her face photocopied for miles, the motel's telephone number written along her chin, just below the word RE-WARD.

Thirty-six inches of accumulated rainwater. Barely even three feet deep. That algae was so thick, you couldn't see through it. The bottom wasn't even there.

There's no telling what was in that pool.

One night, I ended up so drunk I couldn't find the bathroom in this bar. So I ambled out to the patio. Standing along the pool's lip, I unzipped and did my business right there. But that stagnant water started to sputter. Sounded solid all of a sudden. More stiff than it should've been. So I leaned over, looking down—and who do I find, but little Larissa drifting underneath me, still wearing the same clothes she had on the night we first met.

I remember waking up to her parents calling out her name, just running up and down the hallway. Back and forth—*Larissa? Larissa?*

Knocking on everybody's door—*Have you seen our daughter?*

They got the manager to open up every empty room in this place, just to make sure she wasn't stuck inside.

This was supposed to be their summer vacation, see? Driving down to Disneyland or something like that. I even knew which room they were staying in and everything. Number 24. Just two doors down from mine.

Must've been three in the morning when I knocked. Mr. McKee opens the door, keeping the chain lock in between us. Bags under his eyes. You'd think he hadn't slept since he got here.

I took him out back, to the pool. Pointed right at her. Mr. McKee just falls to his knees—reaching down, trying to grab her. Water was so low, though, he couldn't get a grip. She'd been bobbing along, floating just below the surface. The manager had to drain the pool, scrubbing all that algae away. When I woke up the next morning after the police left, there wasn't any water left. Completely empty.

I would've slept the day away if there hadn't been this knock at my door. I answered it, half-asleep, finding Mr. McKee standing there. Not saying anything. He pulls out his wallet and starts writing me a *check*. Ripped it out and hands it over.

Thank you, he says. Just turns around and leaves.

I look down, only to find more zeros in my hand than I've ever seen. *Twenty-five thousand dollars.* All for finding little Larissa McKee. No questions asked.

This was a sign, I said. Little Larissa was my saving grace. My guardian angel. She was looking down on me from heaven, I was sure of it. Telling me—*Take this reward money, mister. Make a better life for yourself, please . . .*

The bank teller nearly dropped her jaw when I cashed that check, wanting it all in my hand. Couldn't even fit the wad in my pocket, it was that thick. Had to carry it in this envelope wherever I went.

The McKees were gone by the time I got back. They'd checked out of their room. Station wagon wasn't in the parking lot anymore.

Place felt empty without them.

First place I go is straight to the front desk. I lay down a crisp hundred-dollar bill in front of the manager. Down payment for the next couple months.

Next I come here, sitting in this very stool. I drop another hundred onto the bar, buying drinks for everybody.

We kept this place open all night, didn't we? Fed fifty dollars into that jukebox alone, playing every damn song on it.

Toasted Larissa every time, raising a glass to that girl. She'd made me the richest man this motel's ever had the pleasure of patronizing. I was king of this motor court. *Drinks are on me!* Tipping as if there were no tomorrow.

Woke up in a different room the next day. They look all the same when you're stumbling back from the bar. Lord knows how I even got inside.

Wasn't until I opened the door and saw the number that it struck me.

This was Larissa's room. Number 24.

First full day with my reward money, I went to the department store. Bought a brand-new suit for a brand-new man. Navy blue. *Pin*-striped. Silver cuff links and a red silk tie. Walking back to the motel, I saw Larissa's face still stapled to all these telephone poles. Rain had seeped into each flyer—her cheeks sagging, her eyes drooping. She looked older, as if she'd grown up in those photocopies.

Wore my new suit to the bar, turning heads toward me.

Look who's back, everybody! This round's on me!

To Larissa . . . Over and over again.

Funny if you think about it, but—with water, it's got to keep moving. The moment it settles somewhere, it begins to fester. *Congeal.* Algae thickens it up. Grows all green. Stiffens and stinks. What used to be fluid and formless becomes all thick and sticky. What used to be clean and clear becomes so murky, there's no finding your way through it anymore.

To Larissa . . .

My guardian angel.

To Larissa . . .

My saving grace.

To Larissa.

To Larissa.

To Larissa.

She's with me in my sleep. She's with me in my dreams. Every time I close my eyes, she finds me. Her reward money's drowning me.

It's taken me months to make my way to this last sip. One more swallow and I've paid my debt.

Cheers.

Hey . . . how about another round, bartender?

You mind putting this one on my tab?

hobo sterno

Three teenagers charged with the torching murder of a homeless man shot a video of the alleged killing . . .

—ASSOCIATED PRESS, 2004

Guess you've seen our little home movie by now. The camera phone makes that man look like a Lite-Brite. The video's low resolution pixelated the flames leaping off his body—so when you watch it online, each digital bit looks like a handful of those clear plastic pegs you punch through a sheet of opaque paper.

Creates this image out of nothing but light.

Orange and yellow light.

The video only lasts thirty-seven seconds. That's it. You can hear Mike laughing his ass off from behind the camera, keeping the flames in frame.

If you squint, you can catch about half of Jerry's face for this split millisecond.

Me—I'm the only one you can see clearly. Captured on camera. I'm standing close enough that my face is actually glowing from the fire, all pink-cheeked.

Press pause right then and you can see I'm smiling.

Just watching that bum burn.

Jerry stashes his fuel cans in the cargo hold of his mom's Dodge. Gives the whole car this reek of gasoline by the end of the week. That and grass. Freshly cut grass. The blades cling to our heels like a choir of clipped tongues, green and singing—*Gettin' messed up on fertilizer on a Friday night!*

We all work for the same crappy-ass landscaping company, mowing these motherhumpers' yards for five bucks an hour—so by Friday night, when the three of us head back into their neighborhoods ready to blow off some steam with my Chase Utley model maple baseball bat, the inside of Jerry's mom's minivan smells like the underbelly of a lawn mower. Nothing but mulch and petroleum.

We keep the windows rolled up for as long as our lungs allow, getting all light-headed from huffing the stuff. Fumes of fossil fuel. Decomposing grass. Our eyes sting with gasoline. The backs of our throats burn from breathing diesel.

Look at this wasteland outside our windshield.

Look at all these McMansions with their manicured lawns.

Their mailboxes.

Nothing but an endless stretch of T-ball tees lined right on down the block.

Batter up!

Whoever sits shotgun gets to hit first. Jerry will ease up on the accelerator long enough for me or Mike to step up to the plate and take a swing. Crack open a couple mailboxes.

I'm busting skulls tonight. I'm imagining the heads of every homeowner perched on each post. Just a long winding row of decapitated nagging housewives all stuck on a stake. Those red retractable flags are nothing but tongues lagging out from their half-open mouths.

Extra points for hitting a mailbox with some mail still in it. Let the pulp of postage shower on down. Let the addressed fragments of their scalps scatter across the asphalt.

Home run! Going, going—gone!

We're celebrating tonight. We realized the world owes us nothing. No matter how well we do in school or what colleges we get accepted into—the best we can ever expect out of life is a house where some dumbshit kid mows our lawn for us, where our own wives will make a pass at him behind our backs, where our children will act like they're better than him all because they were born into this stupid neighborhood.

So to hell with it.

Let's burn it all to the ground. The whole suburb. Incinerate every last house.

Let these families wake up in flames for all we care, their very beds nothing but embers now. The charred imprint of their bodies will scorch through their impeccable lawns, leaving a mark for us to mow over in the morning, until there's nothing, nothing left of them on this earth. Just ashes in the grass.

Smile for the camera, Mike says, holding his cell phone up to me.

On camera, you can hear me say—*Get that thing outta my face.*

As soon as we pull up to the park, we see one of them sprawled along a bench. The odor coming off of him smells like he's marinated himself in malt liquor.

Wake up, mister, Jerry says, prodding him with the baseball bat. *Hey, wake up!*

We use booze as bait. Promise him a couple bucks to go buy himself some beer. All he needs to do is dance for the camera.

And he does it! Just like that, this guy's on his feet, doing this little soft-shoe, tap-dancing with a pair of plastic bags wrapped around each heel. Clumsy as ever, but this guy don't care. He doesn't have a care in the world, save for the 40-ounce coming his way.

Check this guy out, Mike says, busting a gut. *We got ourselves a homeless Al Jolson here!*

I don't even realize Jerry's gone back to the van to get the gas can until he's dumping it over the man's head. Just rushes right up to him as he's dancing, splashing gas straight into his face. Soaks into his clothes. His beard. It's dripping off his whiskers, all matted down now.

I can see he's trying to blink the sting out of his eyes. These dull blue eyes with some kind of milky film coating over them, like oysters settled into each socket.

I can see he's missing some teeth. A couple up front. He's sputtering now—*Puh-lease don't. Puh-lease.* His lips press together and peel apart for each *P*, spitting dribbles of gas back into the air—

Puh-lease don't. Puh-lease.

But he's still dancing. This guy hasn't stopped doing his little jig for us. He's even doing it faster now, *harder.* You can hear the crackle of plastic coming from beneath his feet, pleading with each step—*Puh-lease don't. Puh-lease.*

Jerry pulls out a box of wooden matches from his pocket, rattling them in his hand while this guy keeps on doing his little two-step begging. Begging for his life.

You call this living? Jerry asks back, striking a match. *What kind of life is this?*

Sulfur goes up. The lit match hisses through the air. Hits that homeless guy right in the chest, just below his beard.

Looks like his whiskers burn first. To me, at least. For this split second I swear I see his beard retreat from the flames before the rest of him even has a chance to catch on fire. The hairs curl into themselves, like orange filaments from a lightbulb, coiling around his chin. Hundreds of them.

The plastic bags shrivel, withering around his ankles. Every limb of his is waving through the air now, like he's trying to shake the flames away.

But he's still dancing. He just won't stop.

What's it going to take to get him to stop?

His legs finally give out. The bum stumbles over his own feet. Brings the heat closer to me. I have to take a step back, it's so hot.

If only you'd felt that heat. The very temperature coming off his body. Like nothing I've ever felt before. I see a blue flame spirit up from his body. It reaches right out from the very center of him, burning brighter than the rest, as if he'd opened up some canned cooking fuel and dipped his fingers in, rubbing the jellied alcohol all over his chest and setting it on fire.

Hobo sterno.

Mrs. McCready's always complaining that I've missed picking the clippings up from her lawn. When I try explaining to her that we leave the clippings there on purpose to help fertilize her grass, she says I'm just making up excuses for lazy lawn-mowing. She'll literally sit on her porch and watch me mow just so she can point out all the piles of grass I've left lined along her yard.

There, she nags. *You missed another clump—right there!*

If I leave the lawn mower on, the engine will drown her voice right out. The purr of the propeller blades just drenches everything in sound, endless sound, giving me a chance to strand myself within it. Be alone. For just a little while.

Sixteen seconds—you can watch him ignite.

Twenty-three seconds—you can watch his clothes disintegrate into flames.

I'm about halfway through Mrs. McCready's yard when the mower suddenly sputters to a halt, all out of gas. Must've forgotten to refill the tank this morning.

There's another clump, she says, pointing from her porch. *I'll have yellow spots all over my lawn thanks to you!*

My older brother was the first person to tell me they'd seen it. A friend sent him a link last night, asking if that was actually me or not. At first I didn't know what he was talking about.

You're a movie star now, he said. *Better not let Mom find out.*
Thirty-seven seconds. That's all.

Funny how that homeless guy doesn't even look like himself.
He doesn't look real to me anymore. He's some kind of scarecrow
now. An effigy instead. His beard looks more like a nest some bird
built out of pipe cleaners and steel wool.

The flames swell out from his shoulders like somebody squeezed
a little too much lighter fluid on the grill, that first burst of fire
pushing us all back. Fills up the frame with this bright yellow.

You can't make anyone out. Not at first. Nothing but indiscrim-
inate limbs. Some voices. Then Mike turns his camera phone toward me, my face alive with fire.

Let the wild rumpus start!

I don't remember saying it—but there it is, caught on camera. I'm
on-screen for less than three seconds, but you can see me dancing
around that bum's body like I'm some kind of Indian powwowing
around the campfire, patting my palm against my lips. I'm seeing
myself do things I don't even remember doing. I'm hearing myself
say things I can't even remember coming out from my own mouth.

My first thought was something like—*If I can just get Mike's
camera phone I can stop all this before it gets out of hand. Stop it
from spreading any further.*

But the video's already out of reach. Popping up on people's
Facebook pages. Posted on YouTube. Over six thousand hits since
I last looked this morning, with more and more clicks counting
away.

The world owns those thirty-seven seconds now. Now there's no
getting them back.

That bum's going to burn for an eternity online.

The sound of gasoline sloshing around the can brings me back to Mrs. McCready's lawn. She's got her hawk eyes on me, just waiting for me to screw up.

Look at what you've done, she says. *You're spilling gas on my lawn!*

Look at what I've done.

Look at what I've done.

Before long, there won't be anyone left who hasn't seen the things I've done.

I take in a deep breath and lift the can over my head, turning it upside down. Gas splatters across my temples. I feel it run through my hair. It cuts through the air. Every other scent is gone now, the smell working its way up into my nose.

It burns to breathe now. My lungs have been purified with petroleum.

I pull out my matches. My eyes are stinging so badly I can barely keep them open anymore. I have to steady my hand to scrape the match across the box.

Takes two strikes before the phosphorus flares up between my fingers.

Finally the world around me fills with flames.

So this is what it looks like.

S OFT
T ARGETS

grand marshall

Popped my first shot in the backside of some majorette's head. Watched her skull combust through my crosshairs, this pink mist fogging up the air in between her pigtails. Nothing but red confetti and cerebral streamers showering down on the crowd.

That girl? She'd been twirling her baton as if it were some Molotov cocktail, all lit and ready to burst. The entire high school pep squad's looking like a group of insurgents, swarming around the front of the parade. *Ready to riot.* Their arms are raised over their heads, brandishing their banners in tandem to one another. Whole fucking color guard's praising Allah, shouting out obscenities at us marines. Took another one down before she could catch her baton, watching the rod spin through the air as her body fell to the ground.

We're rolling over Broad Street, heading into the center of town—an entire cavalcade of cars and floats driving down the main drag, turning left on Elm. Right on Vine. Passing the courthouse. Town hall. All the shops. Even the grocery store I used to work at back when I was in high school, bagging these people's sandwich meats for three and a quarter an hour. Well before that recruiting officer waltzed into the back room on my lunch break. Well before he slipped me his business card, scribbling his extension down on the back so that I could talk to him *personally.*

Because he saw the potential in me. The potential to kill.

And well before making my way back home a war hero, the proud recipient of the Navy and Marine Corps Achievement Medal with Combat Valor. Nothing but this ribbon flickering against my chest, pinned to my neatly pressed uniform, telling my hometown that I'd been in direct combat with the enemy force.

And well before they threw me my own parade.

They've got me perched in the backseat of this classic '57 Chevrolet convertible—*Donated by Gentry's Auto, located right off of Route 29!*—all wrapped up in ticker tape and paper chains, an American flag draped across the front hood. The roof's peeled back, letting me sit topside, just next to this year's Miss Rappahannock. Tiara on top of her head. Sash wrapped over her shoulder, like a satin bandolier, holding enough ammunition to shoot her way all through town. Her elbow's bent, hand cupped, waving with her wrist to the crowd down below.

Our convoy sweeps past this militia of Shriners. Their miniature cars sputter under our line of fire. All these geriatric guerillas are tossing rock candy at the kids along the sidewalk. I learned that a medulla oblongata shot jerks their necks back quick, twirling the tassels on top of their heads—so I see how many fezzes I can hit within a minute. I'm plucking off Shriners left and right, like some arcade game, where every bull's eye wins you another ticket.

Bling! Bling! Bling . . .

People keep throwing handfuls of confetti into the air. These little bits of paper are picked up by the wind, scattering everywhere, like a sandstorm hitting me right in the face. The desert's digging into my skin. The particles burrow into my flesh, finding their way inside. Through my ears. My mouth. My nose.

I'm taking the desert with me wherever I go.

And I spot old Miss Rollinger in the crowd, waving her flag at me. Picked her off with a single shot, thinking of her working behind the counter at the Cardinal Pharmacy—where, when I was just twelve years old, she caught me shoplifting a dirty magazine off the rack in the back, slipping some *Hustler* under my shirt, banning me from stepping through the doors of that store for *"looking at such filth in the first place."*

The only kind of girls I've seen for the last year of my life? Coming from magazines just like that. Only type of girl who's willing to give up her cunt to a grunt comes packaged in a brown paper bag.

Not like the girls back here at home. Not like my girlfriend— who kept her legs squeezed tight my last night before I shipped off, sitting in the backseat of my car, pushing my hand away every time I slid it up her thigh, whispering to me that she wanted to wait, to save herself for when I got back . . .

And I remember thinking to myself—*I'm never coming back. I'm as good as dead the second I say goodbye. Please don't make me go. Please don't let me leave* . . .

I spot her in front of the post office, leaning against a mailbox. She's smiling at me. Looking so proud. Like I'm her hero. Some knight in shining armor.

I get her right between the eyes. Her head opens up in the rear, her brains blossoming over the eagle emblem painted across the front of the post office.

I'm a hero, all right.

I hear my name called out from the crowd, echoing through the streets. There's this ringing in my ears, coming from the marching band up ahead—and all I can see are these rows of coiled brass, these piles of twisted intestines exposed to the open sun. An entire battalion's worth of bodies left in the desert, days after dying, yellowed from decomposition. The hollow cylinders keep hissing with trapped gasses, a steaming pile of entrails sputtering up "The Stars and Stripes Forever" for the fiftieth fucking time in a row.

So I start taking out everyone I see.

Mr. Simms my high school principal Mrs. Parker my third-grade English teacher Mr. Reynolds my boss from the grocery store Father Dervisham from church Sally Stanton the first girl I ever felt up Sean Thomas her fucking boyfriend *Jimmy* Jimmy Hodgkin my best friend from fifth grade—

Even my own mom and dad, looking so proud of me. I wipe the smiles off their faces with a single shot. Their lips unravel the second that bullet pushes past.

I'm all out of rounds by the time my car pulls up to the bandstand.

I swear I can hear the hollow discharge of my rifle clicking through the air. But I can't let go of the trigger. Miss Rappahannock steps up to a microphone, clearing her throat—*We're very lucky to have a hero of our own return home today. The marines have honored you for your valor, your sense of honor and duty, loyalty, patriotism, and personal courage in the face of danger. We salute you, sir. Welcome home.*

I head back to my house after the parade. I make my way up to my room, closing the door behind me and locking it. I open up the top dresser drawer, push back my socks, pulling out my marine-issue 9mm pistol from its holster.

I watch my reflection in the dresser mirror as it slips the muzzle past its lips, resting the barrel over its tongue. My reflection never flinches, never blinks, even when it squeezes the trigger—watching the backside of its head burst open, a puff of sand spilling out from the exit wound. The desert spreads over the rest of my room, covering the walls, the carpet, the bed.

Sand? Sand seems to find its way into everything.

party favors

My husband purchased our first camcorder just a few days before Jimmy's fifth birthday, nearly thirty years ago now. His party's one of our first memories captured on video, leaving us with hours' worth of grainy footage. Nothing but these pixilated visions of party favors waving through the air. There's at least three tapes of Jimmy opening his presents. Blowing out the candles on his cake. Even me cleaning up after everybody had left.

Put that damn thing away and help me pick up, you can hear me yelling at the camera, caught swearing on tape for the rest of my life.

It may have been our son's birthday, but it was my husband who was acting like he'd just gotten a new toy. He'd refused to put that clunky contraption down all day, recording every spare snippet that caught his eye.

The moment I remember best is Jimmy playing pin-the-tail-on-the-donkey. I'm blindfolding him in the backyard. The rest of the kids form a circle, surrounding Jimmy as I spin him around three times. All of his friends count off with each turn—*one, two, three!*—and I finally let him go, watching him wobble on his own, back and forth, all dizzy, reaching his arms out in front of him, trying to get his balance back, getting tangled up in the streamers hanging from the trees, suddenly mummifying himself in crepe paper. Searching desperately for that donkey. My husband sneaks up in front of him, trying not to make a sound. Jimmy starts marching straight for the video camera. Aims his pin directly at the lens. There's about ten seconds' worth of Jimmy just filling up the frame, smiling, his eyes hidden behind that blindfold—reaching for the camera. He's only a few feet away from pinning his father with the donkey tail. My husband hadn't mastered the auto-focus yet. He's trying to keep up with Jimmy while tightening in on the focal point, following him through the viewfinder—so most of the footage is a bit blurred. Everybody's laughing, though—these images of children in the background giggling as Jimmy stumbles around.

I can't even tell you the last time I watched that video.

Had to've been years ago. Wasn't until recently that I even thought about it. I had to rummage through a few boxes in the closet to find the tape in the first place, dusting it off and slipping it into our VCR. I'd completely forgotten all about it—up until I saw Jimmy on the six o'clock news, blindfolded all over again.

The image has the same grainy quality to it, shot on some shoddy camcorder. The auto-focus fluctuates back and forth before finally settling on his face, his features clarifying themselves after a few seconds. His tousled hair. The bruises on his cheek. His unshaven chin, the whiskers just barely beginning to sprout.

They have him kneeling in the foreground—while right behind him, there are these three hooded men pressing their rifles against their chests. Their faces are swathed in these red-checkered—*kef-fiyehs*, I think they're called? Made from the same material as the table spreads we'd use for our backyard barbecues. They look as if they've wrapped their heads in picnic blankets. There's a banner hanging from the wall. Took me three blinks before I could stop myself from thinking it said HAPPY BIRTHDAY in some foreign language.

This looks familiar to me, I thought. *Where have I seen this before?* And sure enough, it all comes flooding back to me in that moment.

The blindfold. The banner. The people in the background.

This was Jimmy's fifth birthday party all over again.

Hearing him plead for his life, I remember feeling familiar with that tone of voice. I recognized how it sounded. *This is when Jimmy gives up on the game,* I said to myself. *This is when he pulls off his blindfold to see how far away he is from the donkey, kicking his heels when he sees that he's only a few inches off.*

But the men won't let him peek. They're insisting he keep playing. Shoving the butts of their rifles into his back whenever he stops talking, repeating the same statement over and over again.

When the anchorman began reporting about a relief worker getting kidnapped, I panicked. I grabbed the closest videocassette I could find, slipping it into our VCR and pressing record just in time to get Jimmy. He's wearing an orange jumpsuit that doesn't look familiar to me. It's not something I've ever seen him wear before. Definitely not something I ever bought for him. He's saying something to the camera. His voice sounds hollow, dissonant. The acoustics of the room are terrible, the microphone picking up the hum of the fluorescent lights over his head.

You can barely hear him. The news had edited his segment down to a few seconds, cutting out all the parts that aren't in English.

This is my last chance, Jimmy weeps, bowing his head. *Please, help me . . .*

And I ended up accidentally taping over the last half of our vacation to the Florida Keys. There's about three minutes of me and my husband sunbathing on the beach. The video camera is on me. I'm holding my hand up to my forehead, shielding my eyes from the light—then it cuts right to that yellow and black sunburst, that banner of the jihad hanging from the back wall.

Whoever's behind the camera, you can tell he wants to frame the shot perfectly. Staging everything so that he can get the best composition. Getting the lights just right. Where should the hooded men stand, how close they should be to their hostage. *An inch to the left, an inch to the right. Take a step forward and stop.*

But I can't help myself from seeing my son sitting at the picnic table in our backyard. His friends all crowd around him, all of them leaning over his shoulders just as he's about to blow out the candles on his cake.

What I'm watching on the national news is nothing but some party game.

I've spent the entire week sitting in front of the television, watching all of our old home movies. Hours' and hours' worth of our family's life. When I make my way through one tape, I'll pop in the next—sifting through the last twenty years, watching every moment we ever recorded on camera. All of Jimmy's birthday parties. Our family vacation to the Bahamas. Our trip to Disneyland. Trips to the beach. Thanksgiving pageants. Christmas dinners. Anniversary parties. Heading off to prom. Jimmy's senior recital. Jimmy's high school graduation. Jimmy's first day of college.

What I don't have is his beheading. None of the networks will send me a copy, no matter how much I beg.

Even if he is my son, no one will let me see.

pixels

His throat opened to me. Flaps of flesh trailed in the blade's wake, curling outward, like theatrical curtains, red velvet sinew peeling back to reveal the stage of his trachea.

Parted so smoothly. No resistance. Just a rift in his skin, reaching deeper.

Formaldehyde rose up into my nose. Stung my nostrils. My eyes started watering. There was a sour taste in my mouth now, the flavor of formaldehyde burning at the back of my throat—but I kept carving. Couldn't stop now. Made it this far. Past the tendons. Past the esophagus. All that was left to sever was the spine.

My science partner had run off already by then, screaming to our teacher, leaving me behind to behead the rest by myself. I lopped off the frog's head with one last slash of the scalpel.

This is about biology, isn't it? Why did I decapitate my laboratory frog when—what, exactly? I should've simply been dissecting him?

My scalpel strayed, okay. *Fine.* I've already admitted this to our principal.

But I needed to see.

I'm staring down at the tray. My frog is sprawled out before me, arms outstretched, legs spread.

And I saw him. From the video. He's kneeling right there in front of me. I'm watching him whimper. Begging at me all over again.

A friend from school told me where I could find it. Said if I went to this one website, I could watch the whole thing. All the parts the nightly news wouldn't show on air, completely uncut. Unedited. Uncensored. Just pure, streaming video.

Whole beheading, right there. Start to finish.

The site says you have to be at least eighteen to enter. Like threatening a kid with fraud is going to stop him from clicking on. It's easy to push a button. Such a cinch to click on. Gets easier and easier the more you do it, too. Becomes a reflex. Your finger nearly does it without the rest of your hand even realizing what's going on. Think about all those eggheads in the military. Some geek's sitting in some bullshit room, surrounded by nothing but computer consoles. No windows. He hasn't seen sunlight for weeks, just waiting for the top brass to order him to push a button. *The shiny red button* . . . He doesn't have a clue what happens when he pushes it or who it happens to—but the second his finger punches the key, somewhere, in some country he probably can't even pronounce or find on a map, miles and miles away, some woman fetching water from a nearby well watches this missile swim through the air, suddenly diving down, right out from the clouds, heading her way.

Disintegrates her village in a blink. All gone.

That egghead started here. Awake at 3 a.m. Sitting at his computer while his mom's fast asleep. He's got school in less than three hours—but he can't sleep because he knows there's this website where he can watch a hostage get beheaded. He can actually watch it with his own eyes and no one's going to stop him from clicking on. The only barrier between him and the beheading is his fingernail.

Push the button and the world opens up to you from a two-inch slit, pouring forth.

The video's about three minutes long. Grainy footage. All out of focus. Fluctuates like a fever dream, blurring for a brief moment. Clarity coming back. Sounds out of sync—but I can hear him. His voice trembles, his throat's already surrendering. He's pleading with me. Begging for help.

Hey, he says. *Got a minute? You gonna talk to me—or are you just going to mope around all day? Ah, the silent treatment. I see. Okay. Well, then. Guess I'll just sit here and talk to myself.*

Why are you still there? I ask.

It's not really my choice . . .

Is it something I did?

Of course not.

Are you mad at me?

No—no, not at all.

Then when are you coming home?

I don't—I don't think I can.

Why not?

Not my call, you know? If I could, I would—but.

But?

I don't think I'll be making my way home anytime soon.

My computer monitor is set at a lower resolution. Eight hundred by six hundred pixels. You can see the flesh separate into little dots. The bleeding seems to seep into the computer screen, like when Mom accidentally tips her glass of wine over at the dinner table, the various threads in the tablecloth soaking up all the red. The graphics are guttered in by rows and columns of digital bits. A million pixels channel his blood down the front of his jumpsuit.

When dad's head separates from his shoulders, I thought there might've been some sort of convergence error in my monitor. A glitch. So I clicked the replay button, opening the file once more. Just to be sure.

The sun started seeping in through the window. Morning was here and I hadn't even gone to bed. Felt like I was cramming for an exam, pulling an all-nighter playing and replaying the video. Watching his eyes roll up into the back of his head. Trying to isolate the moment where life left the premises of his body.

Formaldehyde's still on my fingers. I can smell it in my skin.

I hear students have started complaining about dissecting animals in class. *Biology should teach life* and all that. A dead frog takes the learning out of a living thing, where a book works just as well. So instead of picking up the scalpel, they're going to start using this online program called Virtual Frog Dissection Kit. It's an interactive lab. Students click on the Internet to vivisect their frogs now, looking at digital images of the gullet. The glottis. The oviducts and cloaca.

While just a couple clicks away, there's a man kneeling on the floor.

My dad, just waiting for someone to watch.

Get beheaded all over again.

giving head

inspired by the Book of Judith

Ever sever the head off of a chicken, Holofernes? It continues to cluck even after the hatchet comes down, squawking on the chopping block. It gasps for air that has nowhere to go. The brain can't comprehend what's happened below its throat. The muscles still twitch. The eyes keep blinking. There's enough time for that chicken to watch its own body race around the room—a feathery tempest flapping about the floor, every flutter from its wings pumping blood over your feet.

For years, my husband and I depended on this decrepit hen for her eggs. All through the famine, she fed us. That poor bird was so old, her womb so withered, half her eggs were always hollow. Most yolks were nothing more than yellow powder.

She'd been a wedding present. From my mother.

You'll thank me for it one day, she said, winking. *Trust me. When your husband's off defending Bethulia against the Assyrians, that's when this hen will really come in handy.*

When that hen was unable to lay eggs anymore, I was the one who had to take her out back. I pressed her neck against a tree stump and brought that hatchet down. I watched her writhe around the ground in this turbulence of nerves, quivers rippling through her feathers. The spasms lasted for hours. Her body continued to vibrate uncontrollably.

And that's when it struck me. Mom had been right all along.

This was the best wedding present a woman could ever get.

The difference in distance between a chicken's neck and a man's is immense, I know. The sinew's thicker, dense with tendons. But when you've been a widow for this long, Holofernes, you need something with a little more power than *some paltry piece of poultry*. You want the biggest dildo you can find. And you can't get any bigger than the general of the Assyrian army. You've laid waste to the West, from Cilicia to the coasts of Japheth. Your soldiers have covered the face of the earth like locusts, pillaging the children of Melothus, the children of Tharsis, the children of Ismahel. You've destroyed all the gods of the earth for your king, Nabuchodonosor, so that only he may be called God.

You are the prince of my enemies.

But by the time you besieged Bethulia, you were bored with bloodshed. You wanted a change of pace, so you tightened your grip around our city and squeezed—draining our wells down to their last drop of drinking water, starving the children of Israel from the inside out. For a full twenty days you watched us squirm, withering within the precipices of our own home. You bragged on about how you'd set fire to our borders, making prey of our infants, taking our virgins and raping their emaciated husks, as if they were nothing more than corn parched past their harvest.

And yet—the whole time my people were dying, all I could think of was your larynx. That cartilaginous skeleton your vocal cords call home.

Whenever I heard you bark out orders to your men, I couldn't help but dwell on the air welling up below those strips of finely tuned neuromuscular tissue, releasing the breath from your lungs the moment they parted. The vibrations generated resonance, adjusting their pitch along your windpipe, altering their tone with the tension of your tongue as if you were yanking back on the reins of your horse.

From your mouth echoed the words that commanded the death of my husband.

From behind those teeth came the consonants that formed the orders to cut off the aqueducts that brought water to my people.

I'd watch that Adam's apple run the length of your trachea, bobbing up and down—and I couldn't help myself but imagine it rubbing along my clitoris with your last few gasps of air, the spasms bringing me to climax.

I fantasized over this evening. Being here with you, like this. Weltering in your own blood. I prayed that it would be brought to pass that your pride might be cut off with your own sword, struck by the graces of the words from my lips—*Behold the head of Holofernes, general of the army of the Assyrians, where the Lord our God slew him by the hand of a woman! Because he hath so magnified thy name this day, that thy praise shall not depart out of the mouth of men who shall be mindful of the power of the Lord forever . . .*

Come on, Holofernes. You can do better than that. I've heard your battle cry. I know what your vocal cords are capable of. The second your lips split, all the world listens. The earth trembles at the sound of your voice, *so send a shudder through my thighs, okay?*

To think, over a hundred and twenty thousand footmen fall to their knees whenever you yawn—while I can barely muster an orgasm out of it.

Go on. Get that mouth moving. Those muscles are still twitching, I can feel them. As long as there's still blood in the brain, I know for a fact that your nerve synapses can spasm all night long. It took two swings with your own sword to cut off your head. Now your neck's spurting blood all over my feet as if you couldn't keep up with me for more than a couple minutes.

And you owe me.

I came to you tonight as an offering, surrendering myself like some sacrifice—a woman, a widow, my body washed, anointed with oils, adorned in ornaments. There was not such another woman upon this earth in look, in beauty, in sense of words.

And you had the nerve to say to me—*God hath done well to send you, that you may give yourself into my hands. If your God has done this for me, then he shall be my God as well.*

I could've fucked your brains out, I hated you so much.

But instead—I decided to keep them inside.

For myself.

I stood before your bed while you slept, unsheathing your own sword, praying with tears, the motion of my lips in silence saying—*Strengthen me, oh Lord God of Israel. In this hour look on the works of my hands . . . .*

I took you by the hair of your head and said—*Strengthen me, oh Lord God . . .*

My people have promised me that praise will never depart from the heart of those who remember the power of God. My legacy will go down through all generations of my descendants.

But the only person who I want to go down on my legacy is you, Holofernes.

I want you to talk dirty to me.

I want you to order your army to execute the children of Israel, one last time. I want to hear you say it—*down there*. I want to know what that command feels like rippling through your cheeks, vibrating through your jawbone. I want you to use those powerful jowls. I want your lips to wriggle over mine, like worms mincing words, feeding off the same dead sentences over and over and over.

I want to hear you call out my name.

I am Judith, daughter of Merari, the son of Idox, the son of Joseph, the son of Ozias, the son of Elai, the son of Jamnor, the son of Gedeon, the son of Raphaim, the son of Achitob, the son of Melchias, the son of Enan, the son of Nathanias, the son of Salathial, the son of Simeon! Simeon! The very son of Israel!

Mine is not a name that may draw down mercy, but rather one that stirs up wrath. Enkindles indignation. Because when people fuck, they don't call out the name of their lover. They call out for God. The second you come, the Lord's name is on your lips.

So you better start praying, Holofernes. The gates of heaven are open at your mouth. There's a tabernacle in my panties. God is with us, who hath shown his power in Israel! But when you pray, I want you to remember this:

It's really *me* who you're beseeching.

So say my name.

Say it.

the suitors' ward

Paul proposed last night. He wanted to get down on his knee for me, popping the question properly—but I insisted he stay in bed. I was afraid his stitches might rip. One loose suture could send his intestines spilling over the floor.

Better let those ligatures heal up before you even think about tying the knot, I whispered, hoping not to wake any of the other patients.

Paul had stepped on a land mine the day we met.

The paramedics told him to hold his arms like this, hugging his stomach, just so he could holster his own internal organs long enough for me to take a pair of scissors and cut through his flak jacket. The blast had soldered his zipper into a strip of metal, the intense heat fusing the teeth together.

The second I saw you standing over me, he said, *thought I'd died and gone to heaven.*

The men here all call me their angel. Whenever I'm on my rounds, passing through the officers' ward, you can see their faces brighten, their spirits lift. One smile from me and these soldiers forget all about their injuries.

You'd think they'd been healed.

But the Red Cross never prepped us nurses for the number of marriage proposals we'd get. I walk down the aisle almost every day. These beds may as well be church pews, each one holding their own terminal case. My bridesmaids are all wearing nurse uniforms. The best man had his legs blown off by a piece of shrapnel.

That's how I met John. He'd come in with nearly half of his battalion, suffering from severe mortar wounds to his upper torso. His lower jaw had been blown off in the explosion, the bottom half of his face completely missing. I had to make sure nothing obstructed his breathing, just listening to his inhales all night. If something got caught in his chest, if his wheezing shifted in pitch—well, it was up to me to locate the obstacle, clearing the path through his windpipe.

The doctors here gave him a ten-to-one chance of surviving the night. None of the other nurses believed he'd make it to morning—so I simply brushed the hair out of his face, combing it back with my fingers.

He was a handsome man, I could tell.

He woke up about an hour or so later. Saw his eyes for the first time, *this deep green*, welling up with enough tears to rinse the grit from his temples. So I just leaned over and pressed my lips against his eyelashes, feeling them flutter across my mouth.

I held his hand for almost two days straight. Even when it grew cold, I kept my grip.

Most soldiers will die in this ward. These beds will be their last. But no one dies alone. No soldier should ever feel as if he has been abandoned. Not when I'm on duty. That's the promise I made. Call it *palliative care*, when a cure is uncommon—but I have been trained to tend to these men's loneliness. A patient will give up before their body does, which only worsens their condition, so I try to give them something to live for simply by showing that I care.

It's been difficult dating . . .

One of the nurses here set me up with her brother-in-law, who just so happened to be in the service. He was nice enough. Took me to the movies. Coffee, afterward. He even walked me back to my barracks.

We kissed. Briefly, but—it still felt awkward. Not that he had done anything wrong, really. He'd been a perfect gentleman all night.

It's just that you get so used to comforting the suffering—that, even when there's nothing's wrong, you still feel as if there's something missing.

Not that I'm so beautiful. You'd be hard-pressed to pick me out from a crowd. Whenever I slip out of this uniform and leave the ward, I might as well disappear. And after a sixteen-hour shift, I'm so exhausted, I must look like the walking dead heading home.

I realize this has nothing to do with my looks—but more with what's happening out there. In the field. We'll pull out these cots from storage whenever there's an air raid, welcoming in the wounded with enough morphine to send them right off to sleep.

And when they come to, *if* they come to—they wake up to me.

And these soldiers can act just like little boys sometimes. Especially at night. During the day, they're fine. But as soon as the lights go out, this sense of defenselessness seeps in. You'd think they were all afraid of the dark—calling out for us nurses, just desperate for some attention. We schedule twice the amount of inspections at night, checking up on everyone's condition three or four times throughout the evening.

And that's when these soldiers propose.

I'll be on my rounds, when suddenly one of them will grab me by the wrist and drag me over to their bed. Just begging to wed. If he's an amputee, he'll roll off his cot, falling to the floor *on purpose*, just so I'll have to lift him back up into his bed again.

When I get better, why don't you and me run away?

As soon as I'm on my feet again, let's get hitched.

The second I'm out of this hospital, I'm coming back with a ring . . .

The trick is to never say no.

Not outright.

You have to keep their hopes up, so that they'll heal. Most of the time, you're the only hope they have. If they won't pull through for themselves, they will do it for you.

So I started saying yes.

I said yes to Lieutenant Miller, with his torn abdomen.

I said yes to Private Thompson, with three-quarters of his body covered in third-degree burns.

I said yes to every soldier whose chances at survival continued to dwindle the more their fear of death overwhelmed them. I said yes to Tom, who was shot five times straight across the chest during hostile fire, his lungs punctured in three different places. His breathing? His breathing bubbled over so much, the doctor said he would drown before they'd even be able to get him on to the operating table. And when he heard this about himself, *when he heard* what the doctor had said, Tom just took me by the hand—

his chest heavy, every breath whistling through his wounds—saying, *I'll be thinking of you in there . . .*

I'll be thinking of you, too, Tom.

If I make it through, ma'am, would you please come visit me?

Of course I will, Tom . . . I promise.

The turnover of soldiers is so swift here, it's becoming difficult to keep up with my marriage vows now. They keep coming in. One right after the other. When one bed empties, I have a new fiancé filling in. There's barely enough time to change the bedspread. When a patient passes away, I have to wheel the body out of the ward—making sure to smile at the soldier in the neighboring bed, my lips lifting his spirits, holding his hopes up.

I'm a widow a hundred times over.

This clipboard's my bouquet. It's a floral arrangement of ailments, assorted with a half dozen amputees, sprigs of injuries. I'll toss it to the other nurses once my shift's over, all of them scrambling to grab it—just to see who gets to wed next.

uss nursing home

The [husband-and-wife] owners of a nursing home where 34 peo-
ple died in the floodwaters that inundated the New Orleans area
were charged Tuesday with multiple counts of negligent homicide,
shortly after a new dispute broke out between the State of Louisiana
and the federal government over the retrieval of hundreds of other
bodies.

—NEW YORK TIMES, 2005

We started taking on water at the forward hull. The whole ship
shuddered under each torpedo. Tore open the midships as if it
were a tin can. This wave of water suddenly rushed through the
corridors, swatting officers right and left.

Came at me so quickly. There was no time to react. Barely
even had the chance to breathe. I took in as much air as my lungs
would allow just as the water rolled over my head. I had been in
my bunk, trying to get some rest before dogwatch. Hadn't closed
my eyes for longer than thirty seconds before the first torpedo
penetrated our ship's superstructure, taking down her port case-
mates. The whole deck collapsed onto the galley just below. We

started listing to her starboard side. The rudder was wrecked, stranding us dead in the water.

We were sinking. Fast. Heading straight for the harbor's bottom.

A couple crew members tried sealing off our ward by nailing card tables to the windows. People's wheelchairs had been propped up against the barricade. This webbing of metal acted as some kind of man-made balustrade. I could hear the thin trickle of water spilling over their spokes, the flood finagling through every crevice it could find. Their wheels kept turning with the current like the wheel of an upended paddleboat spinning listlessly through the air.

The ship's going down, I called out to Betty Pendleton, resting just next to me. She was still moored to her submerged bed by nothing but her feeding tube. Her body drifted along the surface, lifting up with the rising water. The rubber hose connected at her belly kept her from floating away.

Family members had been evacuating their loved ones all week, picking up their parents and heading off to higher ground.

The rest of us were left behind. Sixty sailors total, all bedridden within our ship.

John Hawthorne from across the room was still intubated to his ventilator. The machine was pumping water into his lungs. His own respirator was drowning him from the inside out.

June Lindstrom used her catheter as a floatation device. She kept her head above water by clinging onto her leg-bags, like some little girl learning to swim for the very first time, wearing a pair of inflatable rubber bladders around each arm.

Captain will have to counter-flood the hull if she's gonna want to even her keel, I said. *Otherwise, she'll land flat on her starboard.*

Well, then, Franklin sighed. *Captain better act quickly.*

Franklin had been the nurse on call for three days straight. He'd seized as many unused mattresses as he could find, tugging a stack over to the nearest window. Placing a patient upon their own orthopedic lifeboat, he'd push them through the porthole and send them sailing into the open water, one at a time, hoping they'd be retrieved by rescue workers, drifting listlessly along until somebody picked them up.

The crew had known an attack was eminent. City officials had been calling all week, warning us to evacuate. But our captain refused to abandon ship, insisting that as many of her staff stay right where they were.

Transporting these patients from one facility to another would be too traumatic, she'd said. *We're talking about moderate-to-severe Alzheimer's patients. The move would be too much for them.*

But a school bus could transfer residents to shelter elsewhere, her first mate, Franklin, replied.

We'll wait for a mandatory evacuation order. I've spoken with the patients' families and they all agree with me. We'll keep them here and wait for the hurricane to blow over.

The sound of their voices was drowned out by the blitz of fifteen-inch armor-piercing shells. They struck the port, the aft, everywhere. One of the walls collapsed, sending a wave of water into the room, swallowing up Franklin before he could escape. The surge pushed the rest of us against the far wall, the surface rising even higher. Quicker than before, our heads nearing the ceiling. Eight feet within fifteen minutes and still no sign of it stopping.

We need to make our way topside, I said to Frances Schumacher, doggy-paddling beside her. *If we don't swim out of here now, we're sinking with the ship.*

Frances kept bobbing up and down. Her head slipped below the surface and popped back up again. Her leg muscles had atrophied after years of bed rest. She flailed through the water, her arms unable to keep the rest of her afloat. She went under and came back up again, then under once more.

Hold onto my arm, I called out. But by then, Frances wasn't coming back up for air anymore.

The navy had been an easy choice for me. The decision to enlist was a fiscal one that I've never regretted. If I committed to a two-year tour of duty directly after college, all my tuition would be paid by Uncle Sam. This left very little overhead for my folks to shoulder, making my undergraduate years cost Mom and Dad virtually nil to nothing. Then there was the fringe benefit of seeing the world. They'd have me stationed in Pearl Harbor, which might as well have been halfway around the globe. When you're coming from Louisiana, the navy may be your only shot at exploring the world outside your own backyard.

You take it, no matter where it takes you.

Torpedo after torpedo, the thunderclap of impact resonated through the hull. With the electricity out, each explosion sent a flash of light through the windows. Lit up the entire ward. For a moment, I could clearly see every other sailor wrestling with the water, struggling amongst the tubes and bedpans floating along the surface. Watching them panic, hearing them plead for their lives, pleading for their wives they had yet to marry, pleading for their children they had yet to father—it struck me that I was never getting off this ship. Whatever future we had ahead of us was now cut short.

Then it blurs. Now I hear sailors pleading for the lives they already had, pleading for their wives they already married, pleading for their children that are all grown up with children of their own.

For me, I saw my wedding. I saw my two daughters. I saw the children they had with their husbands, our family branching out farther and farther.

I saw my wife get sick. I saw her slip away. I saw myself sitting at home alone, the days deteriorating all around me—until I couldn't see myself anymore.

Now I see myself here. Back onboard my ship.

How did I get back here again?

I've been bedridden for decades, drifting about my bunk.

Have I been underwater all along?

I drowned and never knew it.

Until now.

Nearly half of the rooms had been barricaded from the inside to keep the water from forcing its way in. Rescue workers had to pry the doors open. The stockades of upturned furniture and gurneys gave way, releasing a stench of flesh. Bodies lay on the floor, deposited by the waters, either facedown or on their sides. Their housedresses were still wet, the cloth clinging to their skin. One man was discovered draped over the foot of his bed, tangled in the tubes of his own oxygen tank. One woman had been bundled up along the front patio. She was still gripping a picture of her family in her clenched fist. Her wrinkles were brimming with mud. For a brief moment, it looked as if they weren't wrinkles at all, but merely watermarks left behind by the receding water.

Funny to think this, but I remembered it better the second time around.

suicide bomber

My sacrifice will ensure a victory for my people! My actions will be remembered by those who follow in my path! I will be a hero!

I repeated the mantra so much, the words just under my breath all through the evening, whispering it over a thousand times to myself—that, by the time I'd made it to the backseat of Lance Calvert's Buick, I finally ended up believing it.

Actually *believed* what had been hammered into my head for so long now.

I would be a hero. After tonight, my legacy would live on beyond me.

I thought about my family as Lance pinched at my bra strap, releasing the clasps between my shoulder blades. I imagined how proud my parents would be of me, knowing that their daughter had martyred herself for the cause. Friends and neighbors would praise them on raising *such a brave girl* who sacrificed herself within the rear of the notorious Lance Calvert love-mobile. The upholstery was warm with our own body heat, the leather starting to stick to my bare skin. The glass had fogged over, our breath eclipsing the world just outside the car.

No more starry sky. No more cityscape. No more vague outline of the couple kissing from the parked car just beside ours. Life was now nothing more than a narrow path leading me to the next phase of my being.

A cause that's worth dying for is a holy cause.

That's true school spirit.

Are you willing to suffer for the sake of your football team, rather than perish as the penalty for refusing to renounce your school's lineup?

Lance had been asking me out ever since I was made squad leader. He hunted me down as early as our homecoming game. Whenever the Tamilton Tigers went up against the Greenfield Gorillas, Lance would find me on the field. He'd pull off his helmet, wiping the sweat from his brow before nodding at me. That hollow cleft in his chin is as cavernous as the negative space left behind in the earth after a land mine explodes.

Hey, Lydia—if my team wins, why don't you and me go out this weekend?

Well, what if we *win?*

He'd laugh. *What are the chances of that?*

Some high schools kidnap mascots. Others raid their enemies the night before a match, toilet-papering their opponent's football field.

Lance Calvert had been determined to date every rival team's head cheerleader for years. He racked up their pom-poms as if they were the decapitated heads of his quarry. Tricia Carpenter. Charisma Sinclaire. Ali Pendleton. All squad leaders, all from different high schools. All falling victim to the backseat of his Buick.

And here we were. The night before the Big Game. Tomorrow evening, Lance would take to the field like some bloodthirsty dictator, laying waste to our men yet again, leading his team to victory.

All that stood between him and his first touchdown was me.

My blouse.

My bra.

The button on my jeans.

The lace panties underneath. And hidden below that satin, a time bomb ticking. The pressure of it mounting in between my legs. Just waiting for him.

You feel so good . . .

Please, I said. *Slow down.*

Yeah. Sure. I got all night.

Someone else's earring was sticking up from the seat cushion, piercing my thigh. Lance couldn't care less about picking up after himself, leaving behind casual reminders of past conquests strewn throughout his car, like bones littering a war zone.

Ever since I was a freshman, first recruited onto the squad, my fellow cheerleaders had prepared me for this night—where Lance would run his hand down the length of my waist, his skin grazing the denim of my jeans, running his finger across the gritted teeth of my zipper.

Our unit researched his every move. Taking surveillance. Watching videos. Acquainting ourselves with the target before making our move.

I was told where he would place his face through all this, burying his mouth in my neck. They made me learn a list of all the possible responses I could give him—whispering into his ear that he felt good, so good.

Lance. Oh, Lance. You feel so good . . .

This is what I had been brought onto this earth to do. My entire life boiled down to this one moment. All four years of my training came down to this.

I was the chosen one.

I had been hand-picked from dozens of different girls to finally bring a halt to Lance Calvert's tyranny once and for all.

There was no turning back now.

We had all heard stories of his cruelty. We knew what he was capable of doing to anyone who failed in her mission. If I didn't succeed in fulfilling my duty, I should expect a fate worse than death, suffering the torture of my captor for the rest of my senior year. Possibly even longer. I could be scarred all through college. I had been given a cyanide pill before going on my date with Lance that night, carrying it in a locket that I wore around my neck. If I were to fall into my enemy's hands alive, I could slip it into my mouth quickly, swallowing the pill before revealing any information regarding my fellow cheer-leaders.

But . . . pulling a football player out of his uniform is kinda like cracking open a nut. Peeling away all the shoulder pads and jock-straps. Just reaching in for the meat.

For all his bravado on the field, Lance had suddenly become clumsy. His hands fumbled over my body, tangling himself up under the seat belts and bra straps. The determined look on his face made me smile.

Sorry, he muttered. *Just hold on a sec . . . Would you just hold on a sec?*

I could see why girls fell for him so easily. He was kinda cute, in an affluent fanatic kinda way. Having been trained to handle myself in this kind of situation, the one thing I hadn't anticipated really was . . . how soft his lips would be. The smell of sweat was still in his skin, since he had just come straight from practice. When I kissed his neck, I could taste the salt from the field. Like licking the leather of a football. The coarse flavor of pigskin filled my mouth. The taste of weatherworn flesh left to shrivel on the field. The withered husks of those men who had died at his very hands suddenly overwhelming my tongue . . .

Repeat it!

My sacrifice will ensure a victory for my people.

Say it again!

My actions will be remembered by those who follow in my path.

Come on—say it!

I will be a hero.

Again!

I will be a hero!

Whaaaaaat?

I will be a hero. My reward would be waiting for me in the afterlife.

Wait until the guys hear about this, Lance whispered directly into my ear. *I just finger-banged the Tamilton Tigers' head cheer-leader . . .*

Even though I couldn't see his mouth in that moment, I could sense that he was grinning. His lips pulled back as he slipped his index finger inside me, maneuvering through. I could hear it in his breathing, the intake sharpened by the curvature of his smile. Hissing, as he wriggled around.

And then his breath cut itself short, caught within his lungs.

Lance pulled his finger out, holding his hand up to his face and discovering the pin of a fragmentation grenade hanging off his knuckle—like a class ring—the metal wet and glistening.

Finger-bang is right.

In training, we were taught how to carry a grenade inside our vaginas, spending the entire day walking through school with the explosive hidden within our wombs, going unnoticed by everyone. This was how we could infiltrate enemy lines without getting caught, approaching our target without the worry of any opposition.

Remove the pin, release the handle. Detonation in five seconds.

Five . . .

Give me a T!

Four . . .

Give me an I!

Three . . .

Give me a G!

Two . . .

Give me an E!

One . . .

Give me an R!

I grabbed hold of Lance, pressing him against my chest. We

shared the blast between us, the swell mounting from within me and blossoming out into the car, while I whispered back into his ear—

What's that spell?

acknowledgments

To Hanna Cheek. You gave so many of these characters their voice. Now I can't get your voice out of my head . . .

To Erez Ziv, Patron Saint of Black Boxes—and everyone at Horse Trade for giving *The Pumpkin Pie Show* a home for twenty years now.

To Eddie Gamarra and everyone at the Gotham Group for their pious perseverance.

To everyone who ever participated in *The Pumpkin Pie Show*. There are far too many of you. Thank you for humoring me, for putting up with me, for enduring. To Emily Owens, Tom Robbins, David L. Robbins, Andrew Blossom, Tom De Haven, Brian Castleberry and everyone at Akashic Books, Chris Steib and the fine folks at *Void Magazine*, Jeff Dinsmore and Kyle Jarrow at Awkward Press, Jason Aaron Goldberg at Original Works Publishing, Denise Simone and John Glenn at Company of Fools, Hannah Timmons, Craig Macneill, Ana Asensio, Victoria Redel, Hannah Bos, Oliver Butler, Chris Thorn, Patricia Randell, Liz Wisan, Moritz von Stuelpnagel, Bradford Louryk, Abe Goldfarb, Rebecca Lingafelter, Dana Rossi, Brian Silliman, Kevin Townley,

Ronica Reddick, Jarrid Deaton and the *Wrong Tree Review*, Alex Dawson and the *Raconteur Reader*, and to everyone who helped bring these stories to life.

To Indrani, Jasper, and Cormac . . . who I pray never read this book.

Thanks to the following publications where these stories originally appeared:

"late bloomer" in *At the Sign of the Snowman's Skull: The Rolling Darkness Revue* (Northborough, MA: Earthling Publications, 2006).

"b-side" in *The Evil One* (Richmond, VA: Makeout Creek Books, 2016).

"birdfeeder" in *The Best American Short Plays 2007–2008* (Milwaukee, WI: Applause Books, 2009).

"the suitors' ward" in *Hunger Mountain: The Vermont College Journal of Arts & Letters* (Vermont College), no. 8 (Spring 2006).

"pixels" in *Lost Magazine* (New York), 2007.

"staph infection" in *Awkward One: Awkward* (Los Angeles: Awkward Books, 2009).

"grand marshal" in *Awkward Two: Brevity* (Los Angeles: Awkward Books, 2011).

"sixteen again" in *Wrong Tree Review* (Dorton, KY), 2010.

"oldsmobile" in *Void Magazine*, 2005.

"throwing golem," "reward money," and "uss *nursing home*" in *RVA Magazine* (Richmond, VA), 2011.

"the battle of belle isle" in *Richmond Noir* (Brooklyn, NY: Akashic Books, 2010).

"party favors" and "cropduster" in *The Raconteur Reader* (Metuchen, NJ: Raconteur Books, 2006).

"undertow" in *The Best Short American Plays, 2009–2010* (Milwaukee, WI: Applause Books, 2011).

"commencement" was originally commissioned in 2009 by Company of Fools (Denise Simone and John Glenn, core company artists) in Hailey, Idaho.

"commencement" was first published by Original Works Publishing, Los Angeles. For script, eBook, and licensing, visit www.originalworksonline.com.

about the author

Clay McLeod Chapman is the creator of the rigorous storytelling session *The Pumpkin Pie Show*. Publications: *rest area*, *miss corpus*, and the Tribe trilogy—*Homeroom Headhunters*, *Camp Cannibal* and *Academic Assassins* (Disney). Film: *The Boy* (SXSW 2015), *Henley* (Sundance 2012), and *Late Bloomer* (Sundance 2005). Theater: *Commencement* (2009) and *Hostage Song* (w/ Kyle Jarrow; 2008). Comics: *Edge of Spider-Verse, The Avengers, Amazing Spider-Man, Ultimate Spider-Man, Vertigo Quarterly: SFX*, and *Self Storage*. He is a writing instructor at the Actors Studio MFA Program at Pace University in New York. Visit him at www.claymcleodchapman.com.